STUFF HAPPENS

~

H.O.P.E. Anyway

Gloria Brintnall

Copyright © 2019 Gloria Brintnall

All rights reserved.

ISBN: 9781082276736

DEDICATION

I gratefully dedicate this book to

my strong, loving, faith-filled children, Matthew and Ebeth,

and to my family and friends who helped me

through this *stuff*.

Here's to
those that don't give up.
To those who continue believing even when
everything seems to be falling apart.
Never give up. Don't look back.
Take a step forward today;
then take another tomorrow.
You will get through the storm,
and when you do, you will be
stronger, more confident
and better than ever.

CONTENTS

CHAPTER 1	'Twas Eleven Days Before Christmas	1
CHAPTER 2	The Fallout	9
CHAPTER 3	Buck Up; You'll Get Through This	17
CHAPTER 4	The Criminal Defense Attorney	21
CHAPTER 5	Not Exactly a Norman Rockwell Christmas	25
CHAPTER 6	As If Moving Weren't Hard Enough	31
CHAPTER 7	Welcome to Round Rock	37
CHAPTER 8	Suddenly Single – But Still Married	43
CHAPTER 9	The D Word	51
CHAPTER 10	Incarceration	59
CHAPTER 11	The Kids Couldn't Divorce Him	69
CHAPTER 12	In the Dark	73
CHAPTER 13	Why Did God Let This Happen?	85
CHAPTER 14	Awkward Moments	93
CHAPTER 15	Help	99
CHAPTER 16	Another Move	107
CHAPTER 17	Online	111
CHAPTER 18	Full Disclosure	121
CHAPTER 19	Too Good to be True	127
CHAPTER 20	Telling My Pastor and Family	131
CHAPTER 21	Preparing for a Second Marriage	141
CHAPTER 22	Wedding Planning the Second Time	145
CHAPTER 23	Grief Affects Belief	151
CHAPTER 24	From Mourning at Night to Joy in the Morning	159
CHAPTER 25	Five Ups for When You're Down	167
CHAPTER 26	H.O.P.E. = Have Only Positive Expectations	173
EPILOGUE		179

ACKNOWLEDGMENTS
Many thanks to:

Holy Moly Design Studio
Round Rock, Texas

~

Pastor Helen Canty, Way of Life Christian Church
Livonia, Michigan

Unless otherwise noted, Scripture quotations are from The Holy Bible, King James Version, Cambridge, 1769

Scripture quotations marked (NIV) are taken from the Holy Bible, New International Version®, NIV®. Copyright © 1973, 1978, 1984, 2011 by Biblica, Inc.™ Used by permission of Zondervan. All rights reserved worldwide. www.zondervan.com. The "NIV" and "New International Version" are trademarks registered in the United States Patent and Trademark Office by Biblica, Inc.™

Scripture quotations marked (NLT) are taken from the Holy Bible, New Living Translation, copyright © 1996, 2004, 2015 by Tyndale House Foundation. Used by permission of Tyndale House Publishers, Inc., Carol Stream, Illinois 60188. All rights reserved.

INTRODUCTION

Stuff happens to everyone. Sometimes the *stuff* includes an unexpected, life-altering event that changes *everything*.

You may be living right, doing good things, and minding your own business. You might think that the law of *seed, time and harvest* (a.k.a. *what goes around comes around*) would insulate you from adverse life-altering events; still, one day, you find yourself faced with something that affects every aspect of your life. It throws you off balance, and wreaks havoc in your emotions, relationships, finances, health, and vision for your future.

I admit that before it happened to me, I thought that people who suffered loss or grief often "asked for it" by the way they behaved or spoke. While it is true that your words frame your future, and your behavior has consequences, it is also true that you don't live in a vacuum. What other people do will affect you.

Sometimes *stuff just happens* that you could never have imagined or planned. A crisis may come because of a choice your loved one made, or it may merely be a result of the fact that we live in a fallen world. The Bible tells us that Satan is the *god of this world (2 Corinthians 4:4)*. Jesus said that Satan comes to *steal, kill, and destroy,* and one of the ways he accomplishes his goals is to hit good people with *seriously bad stuff* unexpectedly.

Life-altering crises happen.

What do you do? How can you go on when everything in your life is turned upside down? How can you move forward? I'm going to tell you the story of when the rug was suddenly pulled out from under me. It may not even hold a candle to what you've been through, but it surely took me to the edge of hope, where I wondered how I would ever go on with my life.

A dear friend of mine once said, *"Gloria, most people would be drooling in a padded room peeling wallpaper off the wall had they gone through what you have."* She made me laugh. Yet, in retrospect, I am amazed at the grace that God poured out on me to withstand the public humiliation and private pain that I endured. I am happier and more at peace than I have ever been. You can be too, regardless of stuff you go through that throws your life completely out of whack.

CHAPTER 1
'Twas Eleven Days Before Christmas

It was a Monday, eleven days before Christmas when my world came crashing down. As the co-pastor of a new church in a city to which we had just moved 11 months before, I was trying to be the best wife, mother, and pastor that I could. I preached for a morning and an evening service the day before.

My husband and I had been married 30 years, and like every married couple, we'd survived some storms and celebrated some victories. We often worked together singing duets, building a business, and serving in the ministry. Now our project was to establish a church in a city where we didn't know a single soul. We began having services in March of that year, and by December we were running about 30-40 people in attendance on a regular basis — not explosive growth — but we had a core of loyal members who loved us, and we loved them too. My husband assigned the preaching schedule and I did the majority of the preaching Sunday morning, Sunday night, and Wednesday night, but since he was the only one who got a paycheck, he was the one to report to the office that Monday morning. As usual, I worked from home.

I cleaned the house, did the laundry, put dinner in the crock-pot, and sat down in the living room with my laptop to prepare my message for Wednesday night's church service. Since we were nearing Christmas, I was going to preach about Mary's and Elizabeth's faith and the beautiful song of praise found in *Luke 1:46-55*, also known as the *Magnificat*.

I can still see the hand-washed sweaters that lay on our huge dining room table to dry. I felt like the ultimate *super-woman*. I had done it all. My home was clean, organized, peaceful & calm, and on top of all that, I was preparing to preach.

It was our granddaughter's first birthday. I called my husband at the office around noon to see if he wanted me to wait until he got home to call her so we could wish her a happy birthday together. When he answered the phone, I could tell something was wrong. His voice was shaky and quiet. I asked him, *"Are you okay?"* He said he was and that we would talk later. I didn't think much more about it. Starting a church isn't easy; there was pressure coming at us from just about every direction, so I assumed the angst I sensed from him was from the "normal" stuff.

The Christmas tree was decked out in more lights than usual. I decided to add extra colored lights to the pre-lit tree from the year before. It twinkled and sparkled red, green, white, yellow, and blue from the corner of the room. I already had all of the gifts bought, wrapped, and piled under the tree. It looked like quite a haul, but we were on a very tight budget; they were mostly from the Dollar Store. Still, my home could have been the set for a heart-warming Hallmark Christmas movie with the predictable happy ending. It looked so perfect. Little did I know that it was about to become the scene for something more akin to a tear-jerker that would air on the Lifetime channel, full of deceit, drama, and despair.

I was surprised when I heard the garage door open at 2pm. Dean was supposed to be at the office or doing visitations until after 5:00 that day. He walked into the living room with his head down. His face was red, and two strange men in suits were following him. He told me to go to the spare bedroom on the north side of the house and wait for him there. He would tell me what was happening later. It was apparent that something was very wrong. I went quietly into the room as he requested and began to pray.

Our daughter was a senior in high school. The week of December 14, 2009 was semester exams, so she was home from school early that day. Three months later, she wrote an essay about what she saw and heard as she sat on the floor of her bedroom, which looked out onto the street on the south side of the house and was directly across the hall from our home office. With her permission, I am going to share her account. She saw things I didn't see, and she heard words from me that I don't remember uttering.

OVERCOME
By Ebeth

I often wonder what people think when they meet me. There is usually more than one side to a person. There's the side everyone knows and the other side.

People know that I am a strong Christian, a pretty good singer, and a PK, raised in a Christian home. People don't know that I moved across the country about every three years of my school career; that in first grade I was the only Caucasian in my school, and most people don't know about the crisis that changed my life in a split second.

One year ago, my parents were pastoring a church in Lubbock. Things were going well until Monday, December 14, 2009. I was in my room when I heard my dad tell my mother something in a hushed tone. A door slammed. I peeked out my door to see a man in a suit talking to my father. My heart started pounding. I heard more voices. I looked out my window to see two black Lincolns and four more men in suits. All I could do was pray. The cars drove away.

I heard my dad walk towards the room where my mother was. She began screaming. I sat on the floor of my room, crying, knowing that something was wrong. I heard the garage door open and close again, and my father was gone. My mom eventually walked in and asked me to take her to the office. Finally, I said, "Mom, I'm not stupid. I saw those men at our house; I know something's going on. What's going on?" She responded, "Everything is going to be okay. Jesus still loves us." She got out of the car and told me to go to my school's basketball game and have a good time.

"Jesus still loves us?" What had we done? What was going on? My stomach was turning. I got home late to an empty house. Finally, my parents walked into my room in silence. I sat on the floor as my mother said, "Ebeth, your father has something to tell you."

I began to shake and cry, knowing that my life, as I knew it, was coming to an end. My father began to cry and said, "Ebeth, I'm sorry, those men you saw earlier today were from the FBI." I began to shake uncontrollably and hyperventilate. He continued to cry and apologize, saying, "They were here because of me. I'm so sorry. I was caught with child pornography." I began to scream like I never had before, my mom tried to hug me, but I jumped on my bed and slammed my face into my pillow, screaming, "No, no, no, this can't be happening, not to me! Not to us! No!" My father kept crying and apologizing. Words that had to be from God came out of my mouth, "I love you, Daddy. You are still my daddy. You raised me right. This is not going to affect me! Daddy, I love you."

Our church was closed, my senior year was disrupted, and my family broken apart. My mom and I moved to Round Rock to start over. My dad stayed in Lubbock to face the charges.

I am living life one day at a time, heartbroken by the decisions of others. I refuse to let this destroy me. I will make lemonade out of lemons, and my God is more than enough. My relationship with my dad is healing. I am overcoming through Christ Jesus, restored by the blood of the lamb.

My daughter is one of the strongest young women of faith that I have ever known. In the middle of her first-grade year, our family moved from Tempe, Arizona, where we were surrounded by relatives and close friends, to the Detroit, Michigan area to attend Bible School, where we were strangers in a strange land. She attended a rigorous and undeniably strong Christian school that our new boss and pastor founded and ran. It was a blessing, but like most good things in life, it wasn't easy.

The first graders at her new school were reading chapter books when she arrived. The school she left was just beginning to learn phonics. As she mentioned in her essay, she was the only Caucasian child in her school. We didn't make a big deal about race or skin color, but it was a substantial issue for some. She struggled academically and emotionally, but she learned to be strong and tough. Three years later, she changed schools again when we moved back to the Phoenix area to serve at a church there. Two years after that, we were back in the Detroit metroplex. In the middle of her junior year, after she had established friends and accomplished some notoriety for winning a national singing contest with her high school, she was picked up again and moved to Lubbock, Texas where we didn't know a single soul.

It was a difficult transition — most kids rebel against changing high schools, particularly so late in the game. By the time you're a junior, everybody has their squad, their group, and their posse, as it were. Thankfully, a few people at her school reached out to her with open arms, but a transfer student, especially in the last two years of high school, is almost always considered an outsider. To give you an idea of what it was like for her — when I registered her for this excellent Christian school, the assistant principal told me that since she was enrolling as a junior, she wouldn't be allowed to be on the homecoming court. She left a school where she was well known, and almost sure to be recognized in her senior year for her leadership and talent, but now she was looked upon as a carpetbagger who might take a position on the homecoming court from a hometown girl! However, her parents felt called to the ministry, and the ministry led us to Lubbock, Texas, where homecoming court is a pretty important thing.

Now, just eleven months later, in the middle of her senior year, when most kids are reminiscing about their years of school memories together, she would once again be the new kid, and once more be uprooted, but this time, it wasn't just her academic career and social status that was affected.

It was her entire life.

On the night of December 14, 2009, I couldn't get into the bed I had shared with her father for 30 years. I just couldn't do it. My daughter shared her room with me until we moved to Round Rock. It wasn't that I was mad at him; I just felt like we were strangers.

From the ends of the earth,

I cry to you for help when my heart

is overwhelmed.

Psalm 61:2 | NLT

CHAPTER 2
The Fallout

I don't remember screaming when I was told why the FBI was in my house, but my daughter heard me, and I believe her. Here's how I recall my reaction: I remember *trying* to keep a level head, *attempting* to remain calm, and *praying* to somehow find the way forward.

As a minister and pastor, I counseled many women over the years, and I always told them that they were not responsible for their husbands' behavior; they could only control themselves. I practiced what I preached. My husband would go back to the office, call our pastor (who was still financially supporting our fledgling church of about forty people), and tell him what he had done. I've never heard how that conversation went, but I am sure it was painful on both ends of the phone.

I needed some time to decide how and what to tell our daughter. Her father was the one who brought this into our lives, and I felt he should be the one to tell her. I decided to wait until after he spoke to our pastor, and we could tell her together. As you read in her essay, my answer to her was simply, *"Jesus still loves us."* That's always a good reply, and I highly recommend you add it to your repertoire.

That afternoon, my pastor's wife reached out to me. I didn't take notes on the conversation, but I recall her telling me essentially that my husband was not the only Christian man in the world who has gotten caught up in the sin of porn. She spoke words of faith and was kind and sympathetic.

I only remember saying two things to her. First, I clearly recall saying that I was in such shock that I couldn't even cry, although I thought I should. Second, I asked her how in the world would we keep a roof over our heads now? We were barely getting by financially as it was. (I soon discovered we weren't getting by at all. Unbeknownst to me, we were living on credit.) I was aware that my husband could no longer be paid to serve as a pastor. I was working on the common *"Buy one, get one free"* plan most churches use — the husband is paid, but the wife works for free. How would we live? Of course, she wasn't able to answer that question other than to remind me to trust in God, and I did.

I didn't get it. I didn't understand the nature of the charges. I just knew that the FBI was involved, so it was serious. I didn't talk to anyone about it, maybe because of shock, but honestly, I didn't even know what was happening.

My closest friend from Phoenix, whom I'd known for over 25 years, was the first person to hear about the situation besides our pastor and our children. Although we were (and still are) extremely close, we don't talk on the phone much. We've worked in business together, preached together, and raised our families together. When my husband and I accepted the call to move to the Detroit, Michigan area to go into full-time ministry, we left a home I loved only eight houses away from my best friend. She is a strong Christian woman who knows how to pray and hear from the Holy Spirit, and she was obviously listening on the morning of December 15, 2009. The conversation went something like this:

"Hey, Glo! I was on my way home from the Bible Study I teach on Tuesdays,

and I just felt like I needed to give you a call. What's going on? Are you guys okay?"

"Wow. That's the Holy Spirit. I don't even know where to begin. Yesterday the FBI walked into our house with my husband, and he is under investigation for attempts to possess some kind of porn. I don't know what's going to happen. I don't know what I'm going to do, how I'm going to pay our bills, whether we can remain in the ministry, whether Ebeth can finish her senior year here. I don't know what will happen with the church, but...after all, I'm the co-pastor, and I haven't done anything wrong. I know I'm called and anointed to pastor. I just don't know..."

(After a moment of shocked silence) "I'm getting on a plane. Let me figure out how soon I can be there. I'll call you back."

She arrived on Thursday.

Our pastor and his assistant flew in on Wednesday. I still thought that what my husband had done was a minor infraction. Somehow the fact that he was involved in *underage* porn didn't register. I didn't think about the fact that *adult* porn, although it is insidious, sinful, and sickening, is *not* illegal! Since I didn't fully comprehend the charges at first, I thought that I could possibly continue to pastor the people I'd come to love in Lubbock and that my husband could do some kind of community service, repent, get counseling, and this event would be nothing more than a blip on the radar down the road. That's not the way it panned out...at all.

We thought we'd meet with our pastor and his assistant on Wednesday at the church office, but we were mistaken.

"Oh, no," the assistant said. *"We are coming to your house. What's your address?"*

In retrospect, I understand that meeting at the church would have reinforced our positions as pastors, and although I didn't know it yet, it was over.

Our pastor met with my husband first while I sat in another room. Then he met with me while the assistant had my husband sign the papers releasing him from his position as pastor.

My pastor told me that my husband conveyed to him that I was in no way to blame for his dependence on porn. He also understood that I was completely unaware of what my husband had been doing. My naiveté about the situation overwhelmed my common sense. *Well, that was good. Maybe I can stay here and keep pastoring,* I thought. Then the conversation got rough.

"Gloria, your husband is facing 60 to 120 months in prison."

I did the calculations in my mind. *That's 5 to 10 years!*

I was sure he had misspoken. Certainly, the charges, that only had to do with pictures via the Internet, and not contact or violence of any kind couldn't carry that severe of a sentence!

"Do you mean 60 to 120 days?"

"No," he said solemnly. *"60 to 120 months."*

"That's 5 to 10 years!"

I was shocked. It was as if every bit of strength seeped out of my body. I'd never felt anything like it before. Maybe the fact that I hadn't been able to eat for two days was getting to me. I felt completely weak and unable to hold myself up. I slid off the leather chair and onto the floor. I looked at my pastor, who is a rather rigid, formal, dignified man with a deep, authoritative voice (think James Earl Jones), and I softly asked, *"Could you just hold my hand?"*

Our pastor then said that he was closing our church that night. His administrative staff had contacted as many of the members they could and asked them to be at midweek service. He would take the pulpit and announce that the church was closing. The church was too small, too young, and this was too big of a scandal for it to survive. He also said that my daughter and I needed to get out of that city. The press would eat this up, and we didn't need to be subjected to their salacious and vitriolic reporting.

He asked what I wanted to do. I had thought about going back to Phoenix, where my parents and several of my siblings and friends were, but I felt that was a step backward for me. I didn't know what I would do. I was still in shock.

My pastor graciously and generously offered me a position in Round Rock, Texas, where he had recently started another church. I felt this was the right direction for me to go, and I gratefully accepted. We needed to move quickly, he said. Formal charges hadn't been filed yet, but when they were, our family's name was likely to be broadcast on radio, television, and it was.

Our pastor met with our daughter that day too. They sat in her car in our garage so she could freely express herself. I don't know what he said to her, but I know she came back with a clear understanding that her life was *her* life. She had talents, abilities, anointing, and a call of God on her life and her parents' mess-ups didn't have to control her future.

One of the last things I remember our pastor saying to my daughter was, *"Try to get your mother to eat something."* She and I went to Five Guys Burgers and Fries. Her father didn't go with us. I don't remember if he wanted to stay home or if we just couldn't bear to see the grief and pain on his face and asked to go alone. However, every time my daughter and I would leave the house, we took our laptops with us. The FBI had already confiscated his computer and phone. We didn't want there to be anything in the house that might tempt him to get into further trouble. I choked down about ¼ of a single burger. It was the best I could do. The rug had just been pulled out from under my life.

I was told that when our pastor took the podium that night at the church and announced that the doors were closing due to a moral failure of the pastor, the congregation responded with intense emotion. People were crying and shouting in disbelief. They wanted to know what was going on. Where were their pastors? What would happen to them and us?

The next afternoon, one of our precious members rang our doorbell. She had a poster board signed by many of our members. It said, *"We love you, Pastors!"* She believed it was all a mistake, and we would soon be back serving God and His people. I am such an optimistic person of faith that somehow, in the depth of my soul, I hoped she was right.

I will cry unto God most high; unto God that performeth all things for me.

Psalm 57:2 | KJV

CHAPTER 3
Buck Up; You'll Get Through This

I wasn't sleeping well and wasn't eating at all. My mind was foggy, and my body was exhausted. I'm sure my husband was as well. We didn't talk about how we felt or how he had gotten into this situation. It seemed pointless to me. What was done was done. I was certain he was already so laden with guilt, worry, and fear for his future that he didn't need me piling on more. Our house was unusually quiet. I wasn't about to fight over what had happened. What good would that do? I remember one short conversation I had with my husband during that time.

"How could you do this to me?" I cried.

"I didn't do this to you," he replied with a grave look on his face. *"I've lost everything. Everything. The agents who came to arrest me at the office wouldn't even let me go to the bathroom because they were afraid that I'd commit suicide. I've lost everything."*

Our pastor told us to go to the church office and retrieve our personal belongings, of which there were many. We had worked hard to make the church welcoming, professional, and warm. Now, just a few months later, it was all coming down.

Our names with our titles as pastors were on the glass doors of the church building. One of the most painful and vivid memories of our final day in that office is that of seeing a crew scraping our names off the glass door. We didn't speak to them; they didn't talk to us. I didn't know what to say. I worked quickly and kept my head down. I didn't even want to make eye contact with them.

I remember the sick feeling in the pit of my stomach as I went about my business in Lubbock wondering, *"Does this person know?" "Has she heard about the scandal?"* It's a pretty small town, and it wasn't uncommon to run into people you knew at the grocery store or the dry cleaners.

My dear friend, P.A., arrived from Phoenix on Thursday. She helped get our things from the office. She was a calming voice of clarity in the fog of shock and fear. She heard me scream in anger and cry in despair. She saw me in my weakest and strongest moments. It couldn't have been easy for her to walk into the minefield of unpredictable and volatile emotions she would encounter in our home that week. She was truly *a friend who loved at all times, and a sister who was born for adversity. (Proverbs 17:17)*

I hadn't told my parents about what had happened, and P.A. encouraged me to call them. My father was 83 years old at the time, but still in good health and with a clear mind. I didn't want to call my dad from the house, where my husband or daughter might hear me lose it. Somehow, I knew that although I hadn't cried yet, once I talked to my dad, the dam would break.

I loved my father as only the youngest daughter can. I almost idolized him. He was a brilliant man who had some success in life as one of the founders of Golf Pride Grips. Although he knew a lot of rich and famous people, he was just a regular guy who loved God, his family, and his country passionately. He was a hard-nosed German, to say the least. He was very opinionated, but his opinions were always based on a tremendous amount of thought. He had a reason for everything he believed and everything he did. He was generous, but not a pushover. He was compassionate but not coddling. I always wanted to please him, and I wanted him to be proud of me. What would he say when I told him about the crisis I was facing?

P.A. and I drove to a community center in Lubbock and parked alongside a greenbelt. I dialed the familiar number that began with a 602-area code. My mother answered the phone.

"Hi, Mom. It's Gloria. Is Dad there?"

My mother must have known something was wrong. I didn't even give her a chance to say hello. I am pretty sure that standard procedure with all of her eight children was to tell dad the bad news. Mom got only good news.

"*Hyello*," my dad answered with a bit of a lilt in his Irish tenor voice.

"*Dad, this is Gloria.*" So far so good. P.A. helped me write a script to tell him what happened. Difficult discussions are often easier if you have some thoughts prepared before you're in the heat of the moment. Since I had prepared for this call, I thought I might be able to get through it without losing it.

"*Dad, I've got something to tell you. On Monday the FBI came to our house.*"

I tried to finish the statement, but the dam broke. I was sobbing hysterically. Finally, I spit the basics out, and he understood as much as I knew of the situation. His reply was simple, profound, and will stay with me forever.

"Buck up. You'll get through this."

Then my 83-year-old father gave me some very practical advice.

"Get your own checking account," he said.

He would send me some money if I needed to get it started. He would also send my brother, a lawyer, to Lubbock to see what was going on and to help me sort things out.

CHAPTER 4
The Criminal Defense Attorney

I had no previous experience with the FBI, courts, or the legal system. The accused had none either. Our pastor told him, in his first phone conversation, that he needed to hire a lawyer who specializes in *"these types of cases."* I remember hearing my husband reply pathetically, *"But I don't have any money for that."* We didn't.

For about three years before the crisis, we had been self-employed preachers/singers with very few bookings. We had some loyal financial support from our pastor and a few people who believed in us, but I didn't know exactly what that amounted to. He handled all the finances. I hoped and prayed it was enough to pay our bills but wasn't exactly sure how we were. I asked my husband once or twice about one or both of us getting a job to help bring in some cash and support the development of our ministry, but he felt that would display a lack of faith in what God called us to do. So I tried to keep quiet and stayed willfully ignorant of our financial situation, partly because I didn't want to face it, but also because I didn't want to put more pressure on my husband about *how would we pay for this, and where would the money come from for that?*

When we accepted the assignment to pastor in Lubbock, my husband was given a salary, and for that we were grateful. Still, we had debts from our time as self-employed itinerants, and although he got a regular paycheck now, we were making less than half of what we were making before we went into full-time ministry nine years before. So, he was accurate in his statement. We didn't have any money to pay a lawyer, and he definitely needed one.

A lawyer we knew researched and found the name of someone in Lubbock that specialized in Internet crimes. His retainer was $10,000, and he wouldn't even meet with his prospective client until half of it was paid upfront. With a few hundred dollars in our bank accounts, it seemed like the public defender would be the only solution. Early one morning, as I was praying harder than normal in an attempt to hold off worry about what the future would hold, I remembered one small IRA we had. It was in a Mutual Fund that took a terrible nosedive in the Stock Market Crash of 2008. All that was left in it was just a little over – you guessed it – $10,000. We cashed it in, hoping the extra would be enough to pay the penalties and the taxes for early withdrawal from an IRA, and scheduled the appointment.

The lawyer would talk to both of us and then to the accused alone. I tried to put myself together as well as I could. My makeup was heavier than usual as I tried to cover the evidence of a worried, hurt woman – dark circles and the puffiness around my eyes. I put on dress pants, a sweater, and a dressy coat. I wore heels. I felt like I had to present the image of a wife who had it all together.

What was I thinking? *Who in the world would have expected me to have it together? The rug was just pulled out from under my entire life. My. Entire. Life.*

The drive to the law office was quiet, like the rest of our home was most of the time during those days. My husband had not been formally charged yet, but he was assured that charges were imminent.

I had never been to the office of a Criminal Defense Attorney. I had been in a few law offices over the years to handle various business dealings. Those offices were always in the high rent district of the city, usually on upper floors of skyscrapers with amazing views. This, I found, is not the case for the average Criminal Defense Lawyer. His office was small but clean and professional. It was down the street from the city jail; it was surrounded by bail bond businesses, pawnshops, and payday loan stores. A receptionist greeted us as if everything in our world was fine. I figured she was used to seeing people whose lives were shattered and broken by alleged criminal activity.

I don't remember what the lawyer asked us, or what we said. I didn't have much to say except that I was unaware of the alleged illegal/immoral activity. My computer and phone were clean. I do, however, remember starting to cry in that office. The things you remember under such circumstances are often strange bits and pieces, and this moment was one of them. Somehow, I felt like I needed to dismiss my feelings and bottle up those tears.

"I'm not usually like this. I'm really a very upbeat person," I said.

He knew we were pastors, and I still felt a responsibility to reflect my faith and hope in God. I don't think it came across that way. He acted as if I were a little unstable to even try to be upbeat with what my husband was facing.

The Legal Counselor told me I could step out of the room while he got the details from the accused.

To this day, I only know what I've read on the Internet about the charges. I do know there were a lot of them, but they were all text/Internet-based having to do with a teenage girl under 18. No physical contact was involved.

The lawyer told my husband that the police could arrest him at any time. He should not drive the car because if he got stopped for a minor traffic violation (even for inoperative brake lights), the police could haul him off in handcuffs. He said he would request that law enforcement allow him to turn himself in, but there was no guarantee they would go along with that.

Throughout our celebration of Christmas, I continually wondered if we would hear a knock on the door and my daughter and I would have to watch as the head of our household was told to get down on the ground, put his hands behind his back, be handcuffed, pushed into a squad car, and driven away.

It was a difficult holiday season.

CHAPTER 5
Not Exactly a Norman Rockwell Christmas

Our son and his wife were living in the central valley of California when all this happened. One year before, they welcomed our first grandchild into the world — a beautiful little girl — and we wanted more than anything to have our family together for Christmas. Our son was a youth pastor at a small church, and although his salary was about average for a youth pastor, it was barely a living wage in that state, so early in the fall, when we were able to get some reasonable fares, we bought them plane tickets to Lubbock.

We called them on the night it all went down, their baby's first birthday. Instead of a *happy birthday* call, we had to tell them that the FBI had been at our house that day, and despite the situation, we still wanted them to come for Christmas. I think we all knew that this could be our last holiday together for many years.

My children always enjoyed celebrations and family time together. I did everything I could when the kids were young to make Christmas a special, almost magical time, although we always told them the truth about Santa Claus. They knew there was once a real man named St. Nicholas, but he died a long time ago. He used to give gifts to the poor, but no big fat man in a red suit flies all over the world on Christmas Eve, taking gifts to every child on the planet!

My kids were aware that mom and dad bought the gifts. They understood that Jesus is real. Santa is pretend — like Cookie Monster on Sesame Street.

Some Christmases I went way over budget with decorations and gifts trying to recreate that picture-perfect *Norman Rockwell Christmas*. My childhood Christmases, celebrated in a large home in the Midwest with loving parents, eight noisy kids, tons of toys, food, and caroling, came close to the *Norman Rockwell* ideal, and as a mom, I wanted the holidays to be memorable and happy for my kids. This Christmas would be the former, but not the latter.

The silence around the house was deafening until our granddaughter arrived. She was full of exuberance and life! Finally, we had something to think about besides the horrible future her paternal grandfather most likely faced.

Lubbock got snow that Christmas, and we went out to see store window displays together. I drove. We didn't want to risk seeing little one's papa handcuffed and whisked off to jail. We baked cookies; we sang carols. We opened our numerous (albeit cheap) gifts. But the joy of the season was overshadowed by the shock of the situation.

One night, after my husband went to bed, my son asked me if we could just have a "normal" Christmas. He felt the tangible stress, fear, and anxiety. We tried to be "normal," but how can a man who is facing a decade in prison be "normal?" How can his wife of 30 years act like nothing has happened?

My heart hurt for my kids who were suffering as much as I. I wanted to say, *"Sure, we will be normal again. We will smile and laugh and act as if nothing is wrong."* Honestly, I was already doing my best to present a façade of normalcy. I didn't know what else I could do. Sadly, I had to tell him, *"No. We can't have a normal Christmas. I am trying, but we really can't. Nothing about this is normal."* I remember asking him bluntly, *"Do you understand what is happening here? Our lives are changing forever. Forever."* It wasn't the answer he was hoping for, but he nodded in agreement and gave me his full support.

Although the church we were pastoring was shut down, we still wanted to attend Christmas service somewhere. We went to Christmas Eve service at a Megachurch in town whose pastors had befriended us. Their son was good friends with Ebeth, and throughout the ordeal, the pastor's wife treated our daughter as her own. She took her on a shopping spree as a Christmas gift; she fed her and kept her home open to her when she needed a respite from the uneasy quiet in ours.

The Christmas Eve service was different. It was subdued and tranquil. They instructed people to gather in the sanctuary with their own families, pray, and take communion together. Volunteers stood in front of the church to pray with people, and while I felt there was probably no one in that church who needed prayer more than us, we didn't go down for prayer. Honestly, I didn't even know what to pray for! Besides, I was reasonably sure that anyone in that church who knew how to pray already knew what we were going through and had already been praying for us. Why create a scene at the Christmas Eve service?

Most families have particular things they include in their Christmas menu. For us, it's rib roast, a special recipe for Caesar Salad, and particular cookies that have been enjoyed throughout generations. I made sure to have them all — not for the kids or me so much — but for their dad. I understood this would be his last Christmas dinner at a family table for many, many years. It broke my heart to think of him incarcerated, but I was told it was inevitable.

What about faith? you might ask. Couldn't you pray and believe God that he wouldn't have to go to prison? After all, the Bible says that with God, all things are possible.

Yes, God can do anything except violate His Word! The Bible tells us that God established government authority to enforce good and punish evil.

For rulers are not a terror to good works, but to the evil. Wilt thou then not be afraid of the power? do that which is good, and thou shalt have praise of the same: For he is the minister of God to thee for good. But if thou do that which is evil, be afraid; for he beareth not the sword in vain: for he is the minister of God, a revenger to execute wrath upon him that doeth evil. Wherefore ye must needs be subject, not only for wrath, but also for conscience sake. (Romans 13:3-5)

In other words, sowing a seed of unlawful behavior reaps a harvest of criminal punishment. God's system of seed, time, and harvest can't be overruled. I did pray for mercy, but I couldn't pray for no consequences. His actions were not only against the law of the land but also contrary to the Word of God and His standard, particularly for ministers. To pray that he would get off scot-free would be to pray for something contrary to the Word.

I cooked Christmas dinner, but I didn't eat much. Any moment the police could knock on our door, handcuff the man who shared my life for

30 years and take him off to jail. As we prayed over our rib roast, Caesar salad, and cookies, I wondered what he would eat, who he would be eating with, and what he would miss for the next several years on Christmas, Easter, and Thanksgiving.

Our soul waiteth for the Lord: he is our help and our shield.

Psalm 33:20 | KJV

CHAPTER 6
As if Moving Weren't Hard Enough

We made it through Christmas without a knock on our door from police, and on December 28, my husband surrendered himself to the FBI. They released him without bail (thank God — because we had no financial resources), but he had to surrender his passport and was ordered to wear an electronic monitoring device. To his credit, he didn't ask me to go along with him to watch them take his fingerprints, mugshot, or to see them place the ankle bracelet on his leg. For that, I am extremely grateful.

The news media in Lubbock didn't cover the story immediately because the city was overwrought with a "scandal" involving Texas Tech's most winning football coach. If you know anything about Texas, especially west Texas, you understand that football headlines always trump everything else. The coach allegedly mistreated a player who suffered a concussion, and who just happened to be the son of a sportscaster on a major cable channel. To this day, the coach denies the allegations. It was messy. It was controversial. It took up a lot of space on the broadcast and print news. Like my brother, the lawyer, said when he visited shortly before Christmas, *"You've been given a gift. The news media will leave your story alone until this one blows over."*

Although our story hadn't broken yet locally, reporters picked it up from police logs and other outlets. We started getting calls from reporters on our home phone. Someone knocked on our door wanting an interview. One night our daughter went to a youth service at her school's church. I remember calling the Youth Pastor and warning him that the media could be stalking her. He kindly offered to look out for her and protect her from any such assaults.

We got busy doing what we needed to do to get out of Dodge before the *you-know-what* hit the fan. We found a studio apartment in Lubbock for my husband to live in until his case was settled. My daughter and I flew to Austin and found a place to rent for our upcoming relocation. I didn't have time to get rid of 30 years' worth of stuff, so I needed to lease a house that was big enough to hold it at least for a while.

My pastor encouraged me to rent an apartment in the Austin area, but they weren't much less expensive, and I would have had to pay for a storage unit as well. On top of that, I hadn't lived in an apartment since college. My daughter had always lived in a single-family home. We already were making such a huge change that I didn't want to add the stress of a further lifestyle change that involved having to listen to our upstairs neighbors fight, play loud music, and party all night long.

When my daughter and I returned to Lubbock, her dad was doing everything he could to help us. I was relieved to find that he had packed most of the house for us. I don't know about you, but I seriously dislike moving! Packing up a lifetime of things is always physically tiring and emotionally stressful. I had done it four times in the past ten years. We moved from Phoenix to Detroit (who does that anyway?), Detroit to Phoenix, Phoenix back to Detroit, and then from Detroit to Lubbock.

Moving is stressful under the most favorable circumstances but moving under duress is over the top traumatic and exhausting. Honestly, many of those days are just a blur. Our pastor friends in Lubbock met with us and encouraged us.

The pastor's wife told me about the stages of grief, the first of which is denial. I am pretty sure she assumed I was firmly planted in that one because, although I was exhausted, I was calm and levelheaded. I didn't cry or throw up my hands in unbelief. I wasn't asking God *Why*. I wasn't even blaming my husband. I was just doing what needed to be done. She likened going through them like peeling an onion — when one layer comes off, another appears.

My biggest concern was whether the father of my children, who was a music major in college, would survive prison. She kindly told me about a young relative of hers who had gotten into legal trouble and was incarcerated. She told me, *"It's tough at first, but people adjust. Then they develop their own little communities in prison."* She is a compassionate, kind, intelligent, and savvy woman, and from her sweet mouth, she made what most people know as prison *gangs* sound like church small groups. I bought her story, and it gave me some much-needed peace for a while.

I thank God for the love she showed my daughter and me in those difficult days. She was a very busy Pastor of a large congregation. She also might have been a little too close to our family to continue counseling us, so she set up an appointment for me with their licensed staff counselor, a sweet lady, probably about 10-15 years older than I. When I arrived, she gave me some Scriptures she had typed out specifically for me, including a few of the standard verses ministers (including myself) give to those whose lives are in a complete mess!

And we know that all things work together for good to them that love God, to them who are the called according to his purpose (Romans 8:28).

"For I know the plans I have for you," declares the LORD, "plans to prosper you and not to harm you, plans to give you hope and a future" (Jeremiah 29:11).

None of the Scriptures she gave me were news to me, and most of them were already part of my vocabulary. I preached and taught about the power of one's words, and I practiced what I preached. My *go-to* Scripture through the crisis was *Psalm 34:1* –

I will bless the Lord at all times: his praise shall continually be in my mouth.

The counselor asked about the future of our marriage. I had not even considered divorce. On the night that the FBI came into our home, my husband told me in one of our short and few conversations that he hoped I would find a good man to marry. I was shocked to hear him say that. My immediate reply was, *"I don't want to marry another man."* But I didn't understand what he had done, what the consequences would be, or how it would affect me.

The counselor told me about a woman she knew whose husband had been incarcerated on similar charges. She knew that as a convicted sex offender, they would have a hard time finding a place to live, so while he was in prison, she worked extra hours, saved up money and bought a four-plex. They lived in one unit and rented out the other three to help pay the bills. I thought it sounded like a great idea, but I never bought a four-plex.

On January 7, 2010, a moving van pulled up to the house we were renting in Lubbock. Moving is tough, and as hard as it is to pack every little thing and to live surrounded by boxes, the worst day is when the moving van comes. The movers sweep through your home, carrying all of your earthly possessions onto a truck. I think most people deal with a little embarrassment on that day too. The dust bunnies under every bed are exposed, the dirt in the corners is no longer hidden by furniture. Sort of like my life in those days — everything was being exposed, and it was a mess. Lubbock is such a small town that I figured the movers knew why my daughter and I were moving, and her father was staying in town.

I hid in the car while the movers got started. Soon my daughter joined me, and we were ready to make the six-hour drive to Austin. I kissed her father good-bye, tried to encourage him, but then added, *"I'm sorry that I can't go through this with you. This is something you are going to have to face on your own. I'll be praying for you."*

The news that had been withheld for several weeks just happened to break on the day my daughter and I left town. Just as we got on the freeway, I got a call from a parent of one of my daughter's schoolmates.

"Gloria? Is what I heard on the news true?"

I told her it was.

"What are you going to do?"

I let her know that Ebeth and I were moving to Austin and that my pastor had offered me a job there so I could pay the bills.

"What about graduation?"

Then she generously offered to let my daughter live with their family so she could finish school and graduate with her class in Lubbock. Maybe I should have given it more consideration. I regret terribly that any fond memory of her Senior year was utterly destroyed, but at the time I felt as if leaving my daughter there would expose her to too much garbage about her father. I also believed she needed to be in church with her pastor who had known her since she was 5, and who sometimes looked after her as if she were his own daughter. Or maybe I just wanted her with me.

Ebeth became a legal adult just 15 days before the FBI marched into our home. I hadn't thought about it, but the counselor told me to thank God for the timing. Had my daughter been underage when the charges were filed, she may have been removed from our home and put into foster care! She was never in any danger from her father, but the system doesn't always look at individual situations. Government agencies function by regulations and laws, not common sense and wisdom.

Although she was legally an adult, she was still my daughter. The Youth Pastor at our friends' church warned Ebeth not to take on her parents' problems. He told her, *"Remember, you're the child, not the parent."*

I tried to maintain my role as a parent by making her feel as secure as possible considering the situation. I was very vocal in my words of faith and praise even in the darkest times, and I worked hard at finding things we could laugh about and celebrate. We drove into the barren landscape of west Texas listening to one of the few radio stations we could find. It was Classic Country. Neither one of us was familiar with Country Music, but we listened and laughed at the lyrics as we held back our tears.

CHAPTER 7
Welcome to Round Rock

"None of this was a surprise to God," my Pastor friend in Lubbock told me.

I was a mature Christian, and I knew that was the case, but when I was generously offered a position in Round Rock, Texas, God's pre-vision and provision amazed me. About 25 years earlier, before Round Rock became the fastest growing city in America, some of my dear friends from Phoenix relocated there. This couple had traveled with us, worked in business with us, and attended church with us. They had three children, all of whom I taught in a small Christian School in Phoenix. Their middle daughter was the same age as our son. I hadn't stayed in close contact with them, except I had gotten a few emails about a significant health challenge the wife had faced. She asked for prayer support, and she got it. We chatted a bit as she was making her full recovery, but we didn't talk regularly.

Once or twice, after we were living in Lubbock, I visited Round Rock to sing a few special songs at the church. My friends were long-time members of another church, but they visited when I ministered, and I got to reconnect with them — a warm and loving family of faith. They're authentic Christians who love God, His Word, and each other in a way that few families do. My daughter and I were going to need some emotional support, and I figured God, in His tremendous pre-vision and provision, either guided them to move there or our pastor to plant a church there so we wouldn't face this crisis alone! I reached out to my old friend via a Facebook private message in late December 2009.

"Hello, Donna. Ebeth and I are moving to Round Rock in a crisis situation. Please give me a call when you can."

It took a week or so for us to connect, but when we did, she offered any support and help we needed. We landed at their house on the evening of January 7, 2010. But first, we went to church! It happened to be the evening for the midweek service at the Round Rock church, and honestly, going to church was the last thing I wanted to do. I was physically, emotionally, and mentally exhausted. I was embarrassed to see people who knew that the church I was pastoring was now closed. I didn't want people to look at me with that *"Oh, you poor, poor thing"* look. But my daughter insisted. She knew we needed to get right back into the Word and in the community – even though it would be uncomfortable.

Oddly enough, our pastor and his wife were doing a marriage workshop. After an opening song or two, he dismissed people according to marital status. The married people were to go to one room for a class, the singles to another.

For the first time, I had to ask myself, *"What was I? Married or single?"* I didn't want to go to either class. I sat in my seat for several minutes but finally went with those who were married. Although I hadn't even considered divorce, I also didn't feel like I was in the right place. It was a difficult evening, to say the least.

It was after 9pm when we dragged our weary bodies into my friends' house. My husband and I visited them 25 years before when the house was nothing more than a wood frame and a vision. That night, I saw the fulfillment of the vision. It was an abode of warmth and welcome.

The giant oak tree in the front yard was adorned with thousands of sparkling lights. We smelled the live Christmas tree as we walked through the door and were immediately drawn to the fire that roared in their lovely stone fireplace. It was the evening of the National College Football Championship and the University of Texas was playing. I've always been a fan of College football and wanted to watch it, but I didn't see much of the game. I laid down on their chic and comfortable orange soft leather loveseat and fell fast asleep.

The morning came quickly, and one of the first things I needed to do was get Ebeth registered for school. She still had to fulfill a few credits to get her high school diploma. My pastor, understanding the financial mess we were in, suggested I put her in the public high school. I trusted him, so I considered that option. I took her to visit two public high schools in Round Rock, and she attended some classes. One of the schools had an enrollment of nearly 3,000 students. I met with the guidance counselor and sensed zero empathy for what my daughter had been through. My daughter noticed the lack of respect for authority, foul language, and mean and rude behavior. Was this a healthy change for her at this point in her life? I knew she was a strong Christian, but why would I intentionally subject her to this now?

When we returned from the high school visit, I crawled up the stairs with tears flooding down my face. I fell on my knees by the bed and prayed. What would be best for Ebeth? Her father and I had sacrificed for twelve years to send her to Christian schools — not because the kids are perfect in them, but because Psalm 1:1 says Blessed is the man that walketh not in the counsel of the ungodly. I know there are some excellent Christian teachers in public schools, but there are also a whole lot of atheists and agnostics in the system, and the overarching foundations that back public education are not godly. Sitting under their authority daily *is walking in the counsel of the ungodly*. My daughter had already been through such trauma; I just couldn't do it. I couldn't send her into a huge school where the standards we believed in would be ridiculed and debated.

Sending my girl to a Christian school was so important to me that even though our finances were a mess, I had a small savings account that I established years before for the specific purpose of paying her tuition. Of course, I could have used that money to pay off some of the debts that I discovered when I became the head of the household but protecting my daughter to whatever extent I could was much more important to me than paying off debt.

I met with the secondary principle of Round Rock Christian School and explained our situation. She was understanding and kindhearted. I told her I was an ordained minister and that I was on staff at a local church. She made sure I got the pastoral tuition discount. I happened to have *just enough* money in my special savings account to cover one semester's tuition. But we ran into another obstacle. To graduate, Seniors are required to take a Texas State history class. It's only a one-semester course, and her school in Lubbock was offering the class only the second semester, so she hadn't taken it yet. The school in Round Rock, of course, offered it only the first semester, so she missed it. The principle was kind enough to arrange for an independent study class so Ebeth could complete this required credit. The office staff oversaw her work, and it allowed her to get to know some of the ladies there.

I don't know why, but the moving van took a few days to make the six-hour drive from Lubbock to Round Rock. They arrived on a Saturday, and I needed help. The worst day of moving is when they load everything up. The second worst day is the day they unload it all. You're expected to check each item, direct the movers where to put each item, and make room for everything in an unfamiliar space. The movers always seem to move faster than I can keep up. The constant questions have to be answered.

"Where does this go?"

"What about this?"

"Do you know if this piece goes with that?"

I would scramble from room to room trying to get the movers to leave things in as much order as possible. Of course, order is not their concern. Their job is simply to load and unload. As the boxes fill each room and the garage, I always feel quite overwhelmed. I knew I would need help when the moving van arrived.

I was hoping the church where I was employed would send some folks to assist me, but they didn't. The congregation there didn't know me, and besides, we always tried to keep the relationship between ministers and congregants professional, not personal. The staff viewed our relationship as strictly business too. My boss said something about the fact that no one from the church could help me because of an IRS or employment law. I believe he meant that he couldn't force anyone to help me. He didn't force anyone to help, and no one volunteered to help, but God provided.

My eldest brother, the lawyer, flew out from Phoenix, but he wasn't feeling well. We didn't know it at the time, but he was in terrible health; he died three years later from pancreatic cancer. He wasn't able to do any heavy lifting, but he helped wash the windows, and he bought pizza for everyone — which was much appreciated. My moving angels came from our Round Rock family. The middle daughter (who went to kindergarten with my son) and her husband brought the small group from their church. About six young men and women showered us with the love of God as they organized, unpacked, and helped move things from room to room. One of the young men even built our first fire in our fireplace so that the house would begin to feel like a home. I will never, ever forget those young couples who worked their tails off for a woman and her daughter going through a tough time that they didn't even know.

CHAPTER 8
Suddenly Single – But Still Married

I coined the term *suddenly single* to describe my new situation. For 30 years, I was married to the same man. I wasn't seeking separation, nor was I aware of his transgressions, so I wasn't preparing myself mentally, emotionally, or financially to live as a single woman.

That's not to say that everything was hunky-dory in our marriage, but we didn't have knockdown, drag-out fights. He didn't leave the house or wander away for long periods of time, and neither did I. Neither he nor I was drinking alcohol or taking drugs. We were both pastors and committed (at least I thought) to our God, our calling, and our family.

I was proud that we were often the last couple off the dance floor at wedding receptions for being the longest married. We made it 30 years! There was no reason for me to suspect that we wouldn't celebrate 40, 50, 60, or 70 years together until that fateful afternoon in December. Then I became *suddenly single*. I was now the one who would take out the garbage, change light bulbs, and organize the garage. I also became the sole breadwinner and financially responsible party. Thankfully, my husband was able to get a minimum wage job at the Dollar General in Lubbock. However, what he made didn't even cover all of his expenses, so I not only had to take care of the budget for my daughter and me but part of his as well. Looking back, I don't know how we made it financially, but a lot of people helped us, and I was blessed to have a ministerial job that gave me a paycheck every two weeks.

I wanted to take a few days off after the move, but my boss, who was also my pastor, knew that the best thing for me would be to get back to work. I reported to the office on Tuesday morning; the church offices were closed on Mondays. I hadn't worked a job with regular office hours for many years. I had a brief, but successful and enjoyable few years selling real estate, but when we had to move out of the Phoenix area a second time, I left that behind. I worked as an office manager for a few years before we went into the ministry, and I taught kindergarten and music in a Christian school for several years. I also had several *side gigs* — running a direct sales business that grew to a relatively large size and singing and teaching music classes. But now I had to get up, put on makeup, fix my hair, be professionally dressed and out of the house by 7:15 every morning. It was a shock to my system, but I believe the structure was good for me at the time.

My daughter got a job at the Round Rock Outlet Mall. First at one store, but eventually at another as well. She was working two part-time jobs as a Senior in high school. I didn't expect her to pay any household expenses, but she would sometimes bring home groceries or pay for a meal for us both at a restaurant. She was also wholly responsible for decorating my office at work. One day she just showed up at my office with a lamp, a rug, a basket, and a few inspirational plaques that she found on one of her trips to Ross. She used her employee discount at the clothing store where she worked to update her mother's work wardrobe. Her love language is gifts, and she spoke it loudly to me in those days. It's hard to describe how much a new outfit or pair of shoes or earrings encouraged me.

The last few months of my daughter's Senior year were rough. She was essentially a persona non grata. Perhaps other students avoided getting involved with her because, after all, only kids with major issues would change schools in the middle of their Senior year! Or maybe it was just because they were already so entrenched in their friends, families, and activities that they didn't even notice her. No one at her new school knew anything about her. They didn't know she was an anointed worship leader who won first place in a nation-wide contest of high school students just a year before. They didn't know about her leadership abilities and her wisdom in dealing with people. She was overlooked when it was time for the prom.

Her best friends at the school became the women who worked in the office and oversaw the independent study of the Texas State History class. One of those ladies, who knew a little of her story, made sure to let her know about an *Overcomer's Scholarship* the school offered to graduating Seniors. To apply, she had to write a one-page essay describing a hardship she encountered and how she overcame it. Boy, did she have the material! She wrote the essay, which is in Chapter One, and she won. I rather dreaded graduation because I figured my daughter wouldn't be singled out for any achievement, but to my surprise, they awarded her the *Overcomer's Scholarship* at the graduation ceremony. The few people with me and I were the only ones who cheered for her. If only they all knew what that girl had been through and on top of it, she still loved God and her imperfect mom and dad; she was working two jobs, attending church at least twice a week, singing on the praise team, leading worship, and she finished high school! If they knew, they would have given her a standing ovation.

My daughter and I shared one car, and thanks to the proximity of her school to the church where I worked and our rented house to the Outlet Mall, we made it work. I made it a point to arrive at the office before anyone else. My boss took it easy on me at first, but he knew the best thing for me would be to begin ministering as soon as possible. He scheduled me to preach a Wednesday night service within the first month. Some might think that unwise, but I believe he was right on. I wasn't hurting spiritually. If anything, the crisis created a *closer, my God, to Thee* situation.

I think the first message I preached was called *Bounce Back-ability*. I used a child-size standing punching bag with a weighted bottom to illustrate getting punched but bouncing right back. I had taught in Bible schools for several years, and he found classes for me to teach in Round Rock. I counseled women and led worship and prayer. I never questioned God, His Word, or His love and faithfulness. As I mentioned earlier, *Psalm 34:1* was continually coming out of my mouth: *I will bless the Lord at all times: his praise shall continually be in my mouth.* When I wanted to cry, complain, or worry, I chose instead to say, *I will bless the Lord at all times.* How can you go wrong with speaking the Word of God, particularly one that praises God?

As the head of the household, I handled everything at home, so shortly after our move, I needed to drive to downtown Austin to buy a piece of plumbing hardware for our water system. It was a cold, dark, rainy January day. I got lost more than once and ran over a curb with my old car that I was praying would last another ten years. As I was driving somewhere, lost in Austin, my cell phone rang. It was my pastor. He and his legal representative were keeping a close eye on all of the proceedings against my husband, which I appreciated because it kept me from having to fill my mind and emotions with all of that junk. I picked up the call.

"Gloria, are you driving?"

"Yes, sir, I am."

"You'd better pull over. I've got some news, and it isn't good."

I found a safe place to stop. The rain was pouring down; the clouds darkened the horizon.

"Okay. I'm parked. Go ahead, sir."

"Dean was just indicted by a grand jury. There are nine counts. All of them together could result in life in prison and a 2.5 million dollar fine."

I was silent. Life in prison? A $2.5 million fine? We barely scraped up $10,000 to hire a lawyer!

"Gloria, are you there? Are you okay?"

I wasn't okay, but I had already decided what my response would be to any and all bad news. I didn't respond to the information; I simply responded with the Word of God.

"I will bless the Lord at all times. His praise shall continually be in my mouth."

My job at the church allowed for a one-hour lunch break daily. I still wasn't eating much, so I usually just ate an apple and some nuts and sat outside in the sun when the weather finally decided to turn nice. My lunch hour also included a daily call from my husband.

Although we were separated physically and geographically, we were still quite connected. In retrospect, I see that we had a codependent relationship. He relied on me to meet his emotional needs. He would tell me about his difficulties, but I didn't tell him about mine. I listened, gave advice, sent money, and tried my best to encourage him to keep believing in God and in himself. Our conversations often had to do with the case and the legal proceedings. I often wondered if our phones were tapped, but it didn't matter to me. I didn't have anything to hide. He told me about his *Freedom* group — a small men's Bible study at our friends' church in Lubbock that ministered to recovering addicts. He liked to tell me about the opportunities he had in that group to encourage or minister to someone. I recorded our discussion about one such instance in my journal on January 29, 2010.

Dean told me that at his Wednesday group, the leader of the prayer team was depressed. Dean then shared his story, and the guy said, "You're that guy on the news!" The other man snapped out of his depression when he realized what he was going through wasn't nearly as bad as what Dean was going through.

One of the significant legal issues facing him was proving that, although he never had physical contact with an underage girl, he also never intended to. The FBI, who ran the sting that caught him, thought they had evidence that indicated that he was planning to meet with the victim (who was actually an undercover agent). He contended that talk of the meeting was nothing but fantasy. The girl (undercover agent) was in another state.

I believed his contention that he wasn't planning a physical meeting. After all, how was he going to get time off to make the eight-hour drive from Lubbock to Louisiana? Where would he get the money for the trip and most of all, how would he make a trip like that without me knowing? But the FBI wanted to charge him with *intent to meet with a minor for sexual purposes.* His lawyer suggested he take a lie detector test to prove that, although he may have texted something about meeting, he never had any real intention of doing so.

I knew that taking a polygraph was a bad idea. Such tests only measure pulse rate, blood pressure, breathing rate, and perspiration. When a person lies, those indicators usually spike, but a person who is stressed about simply taking the test will exhibit the same as a person who is lying. But his lawyer thought he could do it and that it would take some of the wind out of the prosecutor's sails. He told me when he was scheduled to take the polygraph, and I prayed. Maybe, just maybe if he passed the lie detector, the court would extend some mercy!

He called me the next day during my lunch break. I can still hear the disappointment in his voice, *"I failed it."* To this day, I am convinced that he didn't intend to meet with anyone because he was limited by his accountability to me, his job, *and* a lack of cash. The prosecuting attorney accepted his lawyer's argument that this particular defendant was a bad candidate for an accurate polygraph, and that charge was never filed against him.

The phone calls continued daily. I was suddenly single, but still very connected. I needed to extricate myself from the legal proceedings to protect myself emotionally, but I was still very much attached.

CHAPTER 9
The D Word

In 30 years of marriage, I never uttered the word *divorce* in relation to my husband and me. It was never an option. I believed in Covenant marriage, and *'til death do us part*. We had some very tough times in those 30 years. We fought; we often didn't have enough money to pay the bills; sometimes he had a great job and brought in good money; other times, he didn't. Early in our marriage, I was one of those *rooftop* women described in the Bible — *It is better to dwell in the corner of the housetop, than with a brawling woman in a wide house. (Proverbs 21:9)* I was argumentative and determined. My father didn't raise me to be a wimp. When I thought my husband wasn't doing what he should, I let him know.

After a few years of marriage, I finally started reading my Bible. I learned that God gives everyone free will. He doesn't try to control people. Who was I to think that I could control my husband? My attitude and approach changed, but I'm not sure he ever noticed.

I have a theory that the way spouses experience one another in the first five years of marriage is indelibly imprinted in their brains, and unless they each make a conscious decision to interpret one another's actions differently, they will always see the spouse in the negative light of their first few volatile years. I believe this particularly applies to negative interaction from the wife. The husband learns that when he messes up, the wife tells him off, degrades him, punishes or humiliates him in some way. In self-defense, he gets battle-ready, putting up his defenses and getting his verbal armament ready to fire. He shuts down any receptivity and guards his ground!

After that track has been soundly established in her husband's brain, it doesn't matter what the wife does. She can change her approach, become gentle and understanding, but without a decision on his part to renew his mind as well, he will continue to filter everything his wife says and does through what she used to do. Every time a disagreement arises, or he knows he messed up, he puts up his defenses and closes down his heart and mind. He assumes his wife is going to act like a shrew.

I am pretty sure that's where we found ourselves after 30 years of marriage. I was a born-again Catholic when we first married. My knowledge of Scripture and how to apply it to my life was practically nil. When our son was a year old, we joined a good church that taught the Word of God. I was at every Sunday, Wednesday and special service. I devoured my Bible. I memorized Scripture, and I grew tremendously in my Christian faith. I began to change my behavior, words, and reactions to align with what God said I should do, say, and be. Some of the verses I tried to implement in my character as a wife were —

Let no corrupt communication proceed out of your mouth, but that which is good to the use of edifying, that it may minister grace unto the hearers. And grieve not the holy Spirit of God, whereby ye are sealed unto the day of redemption. Let all bitterness, and wrath, and anger, and clamour, and evil speaking, be put away from you, with all malice: And be ye kind one to another, tenderhearted, forgiving one another, even as God for Christ's sake hath forgiven you. (Ephesians 4:29-32)

Likewise, ye wives, be in subjection to your own husbands; that, if any obey not the word, they also may without the word be won by the conversation of the wives; While they behold your chaste conversation coupled with fear. Whose adorning let it not be that outward adorning of plaiting the hair, and of wearing of gold, or of putting on of apparel; But let it be the hidden man of the heart, in that which is not corruptible, even the ornament of a meek and quiet spirit, which is in the sight of God of great price. For after this manner in the old time the holy women also, who trusted in God, adorned themselves, being in subjection unto their own husbands: Even as Sara obeyed Abraham, calling him lord: whose daughters ye are, as long as ye do well, and are not afraid with any amazement. (1 Peter 3:1-6)

I don't claim to have ever been the perfect wife, but by the time we were sent to pastor in Lubbock, I thought I was doing pretty well at being supportive and holding my tongue. I continually prayed for, encouraged, and withheld criticism. However, I probably over-corrected myself. I didn't learn how to properly approach him when I didn't agree or when things didn't seem right. I just remained quietly *submitted*, or so I thought.

Submission is largely misunderstood and greatly abused within Christianity. Valid godly submission shouldn't require walking on eggshells, as I found myself doing more often around him. It seemed as if anything I said would trigger a negative response. Sometimes he would lash out verbally; other times he would retreat. I learned that his reactions to me were a form of *gaslighting* (more on that later). I tried to do what was right, and I generally succeeded in keeping the peace in our home.

I didn't want to move to Lubbock in the first place. Something inside of me told me it wasn't the right thing to do, but my husband was very excited about becoming a pastor and starting a church. In retrospect, I believe the reason my spirit was repelled at the idea of going to Lubbock didn't have anything to do with the move or the city. The Holy Spirit, of course, knew about my husband's secret sin, and His witness inside of my spirit was repulsed at putting him in a position to pastor. It would be detrimental to him, our family, our future congregation, and the reputation of our pastor and the body of Christ! All I knew was as soon as I heard about it, I had a sick feeling like I never had before.

I was in Hawaii, preparing to preach at a wonderful church. My husband called me about an hour before the service and with much excitement told me that our pastor informed him that we would be sent to pastor a church in Lubbock, Texas. This was great news to my husband! Our itinerant ministry wasn't paying the bills. On top of that, it seemed as if I was getting more invitations than he. We weren't competing, but it was probably hard for him to take. My reaction to the news about the assignment in Lubbock wasn't what he was expecting, I'm sure.

I was silent for a moment. I gently asked if he was sure. He assured me he was, and I left it at that. I went to the church where I was to preach, and the pastor's wife could tell something was wrong with me. As I was praying in the office before the service, she asked, *"Is everything okay with you?"* I assured her all was well, and that God had something special for them that night, and He did! I taught on the Baptism of the Holy Spirit with the Bible evidence of speaking in tongues. The entire church came forward to be filled or refilled. It was a glorious service. But I still had that *yucky* feeling in the pit of my stomach when I thought about moving to Lubbock to pastor a church with my husband. Still, I was his partner for life, so I thought, and I would support him and help him the best I could.

The most consistent thing I did to help my husband was to pray. I wasn't able to fix him, change him, or motivate him, but I believed God was. I wasn't against him; I was for him. We were on the same team! We were one in the flesh. We had two amazing kids and lots of tremendous friends. Even though he spent untold hours in the basement of our house on his computer instead of getting a job that would help pay our mounting debt, I didn't consider divorce. I continued to encourage and pray for him. I thought he was contacting pastors or studying the Bible while he was on his computer. I didn't know what he was doing on his laptop down in that basement until December 14, 2009.

Still, divorce wasn't on my radar. Looking back, I honestly don't know what I was thinking. Did I imagine that he would be found *not guilty* and we could resume our lives as they were? Did I think that he would be incarcerated for several years, then be released as a registered sex offender and we would live happily ever after? What was I thinking? Maybe I wasn't thinking at all because I was in auto-pilot survival mode, but God got my attention and directed me out of that haze.

God is so gracious. You should never wonder if you can hear from Him. He is smart enough to figure out how to talk to you in a way that you can't miss the message! My daily practice for decades has been to begin my day in prayer and reading the Bible. One morning, after we moved to Round Rock, I was led to the Gospel of Matthew.

Ye have heard that it was said by them of old time, Thou shalt not commit adultery: But I say unto you, That whosoever looketh on a woman to lust after her hath committed adultery with her already in his heart. (Matthew 5:27-28)

The best way I can describe what happened that morning was that those verses leaped off the page and went off like a firecracker in my heart. They lit up in my spirit. I wasn't looking for something to support divorce. I wasn't searching for justification for separating from my husband, but at that moment, I knew that in my situation, divorce would not be contrary to God's will. I didn't do anything about it, but God sent me confirmation in just a few days when my pastor called me.

"Hello, Gloria?"

"Yes, sir. How can I help you?"

"Will you be home this Saturday morning?"

"Yes, sir. I'm off this Saturday."

"Okay. Good. I need to come by and talk to you."

My pastor is a famous preacher. He's on Christian television and travels the world. At that time, I had worked with or for him for almost 15 years. He had *never* come to my house to talk to me about *anything* except when he and his assistant came to our home in Lubbock to fire my husband. I didn't know what this was about, but I was pretty certain it wasn't good news.

He arrived Saturday with an assistant, who waited just outside my front door. My daughter was upstairs. I apologized as I answered the door.

"I'm sorry the house is kind of unkempt. We are still unpacking. Can I get you some tea or water?"

"No, thank you. This shouldn't take too long.

Gloria, our lawyer says that there might be a civil suit involved. We know your husband was caught in an FBI sting, but there was possibly a real underage girl involved before the FBI got him on their radar. Her parents may file a civil lawsuit. I am not telling you to get a divorce, but I am here to tell you that you should do whatever you need to do to protect you and your daughter from a civil suit. Maybe you could do a legal separation or something. If you do decide to divorce, I want you to know that you have Scriptural grounds and that you would still be a minister in good standing with our organization."

I know this was difficult for him to say, but I am forever grateful to him for saying it! As a pastor, I never told anyone to divorce. I have encouraged women to remove themselves from dangerous situations because of abuse, but I never began the conversation on divorce. I told my pastor that his suggestion didn't surprise or shock me. The Holy Spirit had already spoken to me about this just a few days before, and for the first time, I was thinking about legal separation or divorce.

I told Dean what our pastor had said. We needed to legally separate to protect our daughter and me from a possible civil lawsuit, and we had to do it immediately. I could tell he was crushed at the thought, but he agreed. In early March, I met with a family law specialist in Round Rock. He told me that the state of Texas makes no provision for a legal separation. The only option was divorce. Since Dean lived in Lubbock, and that was our last address together, we had to file the papers there. The lawyer prepared the petition, and Dean very nobly walked the documents through the court so I wouldn't have to drive to Lubbock and do it.

It was difficult for me to acknowledge that this was the end of our marriage. I called my dad to tell him what was happening. His sage advice was that if we wanted to get back together after this was all over, we certainly could. Wow! Why didn't I think of that? And that's what I told Dean. He still had hope, and I guess I did too, but I hadn't yet faced the reality of what being married to a registered sex offender would be like.

The final decree of divorce was issued in Lubbock on May 19, 2010, 42 days before what would have been our 31st wedding anniversary. Dean called me that day as he always did. I could tell he was devastated. He had truly lost everything — including his wife. Our codependent relationship continued, however. He called me every day as long as he was free to do so.

CHAPTER 10

Incarceration

Nothing will change your opinion about crime and punishment like having a loved one incarcerated. I always thought I was a *tough on crime* voter, but once I had someone that I loved go through the criminal justice system, I wondered if it was more criminal than just. Thank God for the prison reform that our current Executive Branch of government (in 2019) has pushed. I've had a few relatives and friends other than Dean deal with legal issues — some criminal, some civil — and what has been proven 100% of the time is that the judicial system is not blind. It sees very well when money, power, or influence is present. Those who can afford top-dollar lawyers and pay for endless appeals always come out better in our legal system than the person who uses the public defender or is financially limited in his ability to appeal.

Our $10,000 paid for a lawyer who at least got the Assistant U.S. Attorney, who was prosecuting the case, to accept a plea of *guilty* on one count instead of nine. On March 25, 2010, Dean entered a plea of *guilty* to *one count of attempt to possess child porn.* Sentencing was initially scheduled for June but was rescheduled for July 9. The wait was torturous. I prayed. I asked people to write letters to the judge asking for leniency. This was his first offense; there was no physical contact; he was a good man who had done a very bad thing. Couldn't they please show some mercy?

The probation officer, who has the job of recommending appropriate sentencing, called me shortly before his presentencing report was due. I wasn't prepared for his call or his questions. He was not at all friendly and didn't offer me much information about the sentencing. He wanted to know if I planned on getting back together with Dean after he was released from prison. My very honest answer was, *"I don't know."* I asked him what sentence he was recommending. He answered coldly, *"the maximum; ten years."* He assured me that the court would go along with his recommendation. There was no point in asking any other questions.

My journal entry from July 9, 2010 reads —

Today is Dean's sentencing hearing. Judgment day. How I've prayed for mercy. The lawyer says it's already decided. I continue to pray. The tears are flowing this morning — shattered dreams, a broken heart. My heart literally hurts. I'm not even sure who I'm crying for — is it okay to be sad because of the situation you're in but also okay to feel pain for others? Jesus wept. Yet I know the tears, the sadness, the loneliness, the pain will go on as long as I allow it. There comes a time when I have to "buck up," as my dad would say — and move forward. Jesus is coming soon.

Our son and our dear friend, Stu, from Round Rock, went to be with Dean at the sentencing. They told me later that it was just like you see on TV—reporters everywhere trying to snap pictures. They covered their heads with their sports jackets and continued walking — just like you see on TV. My son told me later that after the sentence was read, his father was allowed to walk over to him, hug him, and give him his watch and wedding ring. My son and his father cried as they embraced. Many years later, my heart still aches for what they endured on that day.

Matthew and Stu went to Dean's apartment and cleaned it out. They sent nearly everything to the Salvation Army. Then they got in Dean's car and drove it to Round Rock. Stu's wife, Donna, invited me to come to be with her while we waited to hear the results of the sentencing. Although the probation officer told me to expect the maximum of 10 years, I still held out hope for mercy. Shortly after 10am on July 9, 2010, we got the call from my son.

"Ten years."

I asked how he was.

"It was rough."

Donna hugged me, and I wept. The man who shared my bed, who fathered my children, who made me angry and made me laugh, the man who sang duets with me and bought and sold houses with me and moved across the country numerous times with me was now an inmate. He would be stripped, his head would be shaved, and given shots and prison garb. He would line up with other men — gang members, thieves, rapists, and killers — to go to breakfast, lunch, and dinner. I prayed that he wouldn't be assaulted in prison. I haven't asked, and no one has told me whether he was or not, but I was told that men who go to prison for any kind of child sex-related crime were almost always beaten and raped. My heart still breaks at the possibility. All I could do was pray.

Matthew spent the weekend with me in Round Rock. At the time, my boss was opening a church in Dallas, and he had talked to me about sending me there to help him run that church.

My journal entry from July 12, 2010 —

July 12 — A weekend of grieving over the severity of the sentence; grieving for how I'm sure Dean is feeling. Many tears. Matthew was a HUGE blessing. We had some good talks. He told me that now it's supposed to "be all about me." (Sounds rather selfish to me!) Matthew told me that truly, this is an exciting time of new beginnings for me. I'm still working on getting that revelation. When I think about moving to Dallas and being totally alone — coming home to an empty house every day — I wonder why did I invest 30 years building a family? I told Ebeth that, and in her incredible wisdom and insight, she said, "You didn't raise us just so we could entertain you." True. Matthew said I need to rediscover what I want — that is also true.

My son, who had just seen his father sentenced to 10 years, had the compassion and wherewithal to minister to his mother that weekend. I hadn't broached the subject of dating or finding another husband. I thought it would be too emotionally hard on my kids, but that weekend, my son said, *"Mom, if you find a good man and you think you might want to start seeing him, I think you should."* I certainly didn't have any prospects, and I wasn't planning on dating anyone any time soon; dating wasn't even on my radar that weekend. I was still reeling from the sentencing.

As egregious as Dean's crime was, his sentence seemed quite harsh, and it was. In the next few years, I watched as celebrities and politicians were found guilty of similar or much worse crimes but got much lighter sentences. For example, Anthony Weiner, whose wife worked for Hillary Clinton, pled guilty to *transferring obscene material to a minor.* He was sentenced to 21 *months* in prison, and only served 18 *months.* Former NFL star Lawrence Taylor hired a 16-year-old girl from a pimp in New York. When arrested, he claimed he thought she was 18. He served *no* jail time. We understand first-hand that, although it is comforting to believe that justice in America is blind, it is not.

Before the sentencing, Dean and I were still talking daily. Once he was incarcerated, he could only make calls one or two days a week. He called me and asked for money to be put in his account for some athletic shoes. I thought that prisoners were provided with everything they need. That's what all the Facebook memes have you believe, anyway. They make it look as if Federal Prisons are summer camps. They are not. Evidently, he was given one pair of some kind of boots, but they hurt his feet. However, he was allowed to purchase some athletic shoes. I sent him the money. I don't remember how much it was, but I knew I could have found him some good shoes for about half as much. I was on a super tight budget, and the shoe money took a big bite out of it.

In case you don't know, you can't just send money — or anything — to prison. Each inmate has an account into which you can send money. I had to get his prisoner I.D. number and the information on the prison *"bank system."* The next step was to find a Western Union office and have them wire the money to the account. I wondered as I stood in line at the grocery store Western Union desk if the employee would ask who I knew in prison. She didn't, and I got the money into prisoner #16457889's account.

About a week later, I got a call from Dean. I always knew it was him because the caller ID came up as "No caller ID" Then, as is customary from every Federal Prison, a recorded message alerted me to the fact that an inmate was attempting to contact me. The recipient then has the option of receiving or rejecting the call. I always accepted his calls. He sounded like he had been crying.

"*My shoes were stolen.*"

"*Did you keep them in your locker?*"

"*No. I had them under my bed.*"

"*Dean...you're living with criminals.*"

That sounds harsh when I think about it now, but it was the truth. I hung up the phone and began sobbing. I pictured his living conditions, the men who surrounded him 24 hours a day, and I felt his pain in the depths of my soul.

Shortly after that, my friend P.A. came to visit me. We took an overnight jaunt to San Antonio, and on the way home, as I was driving north on I-35, I was talking about Dean, and I began to cry hysterically. I couldn't breathe; I was out of control. I had to pull over and get myself together to finish the drive. I was scheduled to lead worship the next day, and although I knew I was an emotional wreck, I didn't ask to be relieved of that responsibility. After all, my mantra was always *the show must go on*. The next morning, in the middle of an anointed worship song, I just got lost. I didn't know where the rests were and where we were supposed to sing. It was a train wreck. Somehow, I finished the worship set and practically ran off stage to the back of the auditorium. That was the last day I ever led worship.

As you might imagine, the worship train wreck elicited a meeting with my pastor. First, he wasn't happy with the train wreck. Second, he knew that wasn't like me, and something must be wrong. When I told him about the shoes, the phone calls, and the images playing in my head of how my former husband was suffering, he asked if I wanted to be married to him again.

"I don't know," I answered honestly.

"Do you still love him?" my pastor asked.

"I don't know. I guess so. I mean, we were married for 30 years, but I really don't know."

Then he said one of the wisest things I've ever heard.

"You know it's possible to love more than one person. I have married couples who were widowed or divorced, and they still had a love for their first spouse."

I had never heard of such a thing, nor had I thought such a thought! But that one sentence set me free!

"So, what do you want, Gloria?"

I honestly didn't know. I hadn't thought much about what I wanted, only about what he and everyone else needed.

Then my pastor made a tremendously insightful suggestion.

"You need to cut off communication with him for at least six months."

My pastor realized the codependent relationship that held me captive.

"After six months, you'll know if you want a future with him. If you don't,

then you need to let him know and cut off further communication too."

That's what I did. I let Dean know what I was doing and why I was doing it. The kids stayed in touch with him and served as an intermediary if we needed to get information back and forth between one another. I wish I could say that those six months were difficult for me, but they weren't. They were a respite. I finally could focus on my life and future. I didn't continually imagine what his life was like. I stopped putting myself emotionally in prison with him — feeling the weight of his sentence as if it were my own.

As I prayed about my future and his, the Holy Spirit revealed to me that I couldn't pay for my former husband's crime, and I shouldn't be expected to. If I remained emotionally attached to him, I would continue to agonize hearing about his suffering. Furthermore, the Holy Spirit showed me that I would be a terrible wife for him after ten years in prison. The Lord said He knew that I would *try* to be kind and understanding, but I would be married to a registered sex offender. Unless we came into some serious money and could purchase a house, renting one would be almost impossible. He wouldn't be able to get a job, and I would be the one who would have to financially support the home. It wouldn't be a healthy or happy situation for him or me.

Six months after our imposed phone separation, I told my son to give his dad the day and time to call me. P.A., who'd helped me write the words for telling my dad what happened, also helped me put together a short, to-the-point script for giving Dean the sad news. I went to my friend's house in Round Rock, and Donna prayed me through that morning. It may sound cold, but I had to make the message clear and honest for his sake as well as mine. The script went something like this:

"Thank you for calling and for abiding by my request for the last six months. I will always honor you as the father of my children, but I don't see any future for you and me, so please don't call me anymore."

He was choked up, but he acknowledged that he understood, and we hung up. That was the last I spoke to him.

How long must I struggle with anguish in my soul, with sorrow in my heart every day?

Psalm 13:2 | NLT

CHAPTER 11
The Kids Couldn't Divorce Him

My life got easier when I severed ties with my former husband, but my kids' lives didn't. There was no legal way for them to separate themselves from their father. Although he has two living brothers, they didn't interact with him much before he was incarcerated, much less after. A few generous and kind people from the church wrote to him and put money in his account periodically, but the only regular connection to the outside world he had was his kids.

Sometime in May, our pastor arranged to take Ebeth to visit her father. He was incarcerated in Big Spring, Texas which is in the middle of nowhere over near Lubbock, which is in the west part of…nowhere. It's a long drive from Austin. Our pastor arranged for a plane to fly him and my daughter from Dallas to Big Spring. Ebeth and I drove to Dallas since I was preparing to move there and had to be there to manage Sunday service the next day. An employee from the church gave us a ride to DFW airport. I sent her off with a hug and a prayer. The church employee asked me if I was okay. I was worried about my precious girl. I knew she was strong, but I couldn't imagine what it would be like to see your father locked up in a Federal Penitentiary. I tried to keep a happy demeanor as she went on her way, but my heart was heavy.

I'm not sure how it happened, but I ended up going to the spa that day. I can't remember if someone booked it for me or if I decided to do it as a distraction. Either way, when Ebeth returned to Dallas, she met me at the spa, and we had dinner together at a Mexican restaurant nearby. She laughed at the irony of her day.

"*You know, this is the kind of thing reality shows are made of.*"

"What do you mean?" I asked.

"*Mother.*" She rolled her eyes. "*I visited my father in prison and then met my mother at the spa. Who does that?*"

She was right. It was odd. But at least we always tried to keep a sense of humor about what was happening.

She told me very little about the visit except that the prison system doesn't make visiting easy — at all. She had to submit her name and other personal information several weeks in advance so she could be cleared to get in. Visiting days are Saturday and Sunday only. She couldn't take her phone or any electronics with her. She had to go through security. The wire in her bra set off the alarm. They wouldn't let her in until an officer discarded that wire.

"*There I was,*" she told me, "*people standing around watching as I was trying to remove the wire from my bra with a pair of office scissors!*"

My kids treated me with the utmost sensitivity and consideration. They knew it was hard on me to hear about how their dad was hurting, so they kept all that information to themselves. I didn't hear much else about her visit, but I know it was difficult.

My son and his wife moved from California back to the Detroit area shortly after Dean's incarceration. In March of 2013, their family had grown to include not one, but three beautiful girls, and they were transferred to the Dallas church, where I had moved a few years earlier. It was so nice for me to finally have some family in Dallas! Once they resided in Texas, they committed to visiting his father at least once a year. That may not sound like much to you, but the effort to take three little girls to visit their grandfather in prison in Big Spring, Texas was significant! It's at least a 6-hour drive, and with Saturday and Sunday being the only visiting days, it was difficult for my son, who is a pastor, to get away on a weekend. Still, they packed up those three precious little girls and made the trip across Texas. They would leave Dallas on Friday; spend the night at a hotel in Midland Friday night, then get on the road early Saturday morning so they would get to the prison in plenty of time to make visiting hours. God bless my daughter-in-law. She didn't sign up for this when she married my son! I fully expect the blessing of *Ephesians 6:2-3* to manifest in both my son's as well as my daughter's family. They have honored their father in a way that few adult children would.

I asked my daughter-in-law once what they told the girls about their *Papa T*, as they call him. *"We just say that's where he works and he can't get away to see us, so we go see him."*

Since he and I had cut off communications, he called the kids every week, at least he tried. They couldn't always pick up, sometimes because they were busy, sometimes because they weren't emotionally ready to talk. It was difficult to hear what he was going through and of the dangerous and unjust situations. At one point, the prison had a new warden who wasn't right, just, or fair. Things were being stolen from the inmates' lockers. It was most likely the work of some of the guards, but nothing was done. How can prisoners do anything about the guards stealing stuff? My kids were angry and frustrated. They had given their dad money to buy an iPod on which he could listen to music and preaching, and it was stolen. The prison system is a mess. In high school government class, we learned that *"absolute power corrupts absolutely,"* and nowhere is that more accurate than the prison system.

Although my kids played everything very close to the vest when it came to information about their dad, my daughter-in-law would often tip me off about what was going on. She was the one who told me about the warden situation. She also told me that her father-in-law's job inside the prison was that of a teacher. His college degree was an asset in prison — not too many of his neighbors had one. He also got His Ph.D. in religious studies while he was there. It's a good thing I wasn't involved. I would have told him to learn a more marketable trade like welding or plumbing. Still, having a doctorate is an achievement that most, including me, have not accomplished, and for that, I am happy for him.

CHAPTER 12
In the Dark

My situation was rather unique. Most people whose marriages are on the brink exhibit some indicators, but I didn't have any forewarnings about the impending destruction of my marriage, home, and ministry. We weren't fighting or arguing. He was home for dinner with our daughter and me every night. He went to the office every day and was in church every Sunday and Wednesday. Everything seemed just fine.

Out of nowhere — like a bolt of lightning — my life changed in a split second. Sunday, I was the stable wife of 30 years, an anointed preacher and pastor joyfully flowing in my calling. On Monday, I was the soon-to-be ex-wife of a soon-to-be registered sex offender. It was so sudden, shocking, and life-altering that I often liken it to getting the news that someone you love just died. No one gets up in the morning, expecting that their loved one will perish in a freak accident. I certainly didn't wake up on December 14, 2009, thinking that the FBI might walk into my house that day and my life would be forever changed.

I didn't know what my husband was doing. I wasn't aware that he was addicted to porn and essentially a sex addict, which he finally admitted to me after his arrest. I remember the phone call when he told me he had been to see a wonderful, wise, older man who was counseling him at our friend's church in Lubbock. He told me that this dear saintly gentleman asked him bluntly, *"Are you addicted to sex?"* Dean said he paused and then admitted that he was.

You may think if anyone knows a man is a sex addict, it would be his wife, right? We had a normal and (I thought) fulfilling intimate relationship. Without going into more detail than I should, let me just say that I never refused my husband his *due benevolence (1 Corinthians 7:3)*. So, the question often arises, *"How could you not have known what your husband was doing?"*

Hindsight is always 20/20, especially when it comes to dealing with addictive behavior. When I look back on some things, I now think, *"I should have known."* For example, we both had our own laptops and phones. I remember one day when I tried to get into his computer, and he had changed the password. I called him and asked for the new password. He gave me a password, but of course, that didn't work either. He said I must have done something wrong and he would look at it when he got home. That should have been a clue, but I missed it.

Our marriage wasn't perfect; I honestly don't know any that are, but our home was calm. Our early years of marriage were more tumultuous partially because of my strong personality, high expectations, and Germanic work ethic. When, in our later years, he became quieter and more defensive, I assumed that his negative reactions to my questions or concerns were simply his defense against a possible flare-up of my past strong-willed behavior, or perhaps it was merely a part of the normal aging process.

I understand now that his passive-aggressive behavior towards me in the last few years of our marriage was what counselors call *gaslighting*. For example, if I asked, *"What are you working on in the basement?"* or any such question, he would sharply reply, *"I'm working. What do you think I'm doing?"* He would accuse me of not believing in him or not walking in faith. Whether he did it intentionally or not, he knew I would do almost anything to keep the peace in our house, so when he would puff up at my inquiries, I wouldn't ask any more questions. I would stop digging, apologize, and work on my attitude.

To this day, he may not even be aware of the term *gaslighting*, but he was very good at it. Psychologists and counselors say that all addicts become well-versed in its practices because it helps them hide their behavior. It is a form of manipulation that makes the partner feel as if he/she is imagining a problem that simply does not exist. After a while, the non-addict partner begins to feel as if he/she is crazy or entirely in the wrong.

Due to such manipulation, I found myself offering contrition for asking him what he was doing in the basement on his computer. I didn't suspect he was looking at porn or visiting illicit chat rooms. Honestly, I just wanted to know what was happening with our ministry. Was he contacting pastors? Did he book us to sing or preach anywhere? Do we need to connect with our partners? Should I send out a newsletter? Have you found any place where we could serve our community? I knew that we were not making much forward progress, although I did whatever I could on my own. I arranged to minister weekly at a soup kitchen in the Brightmoor district of Detroit. I also volunteered my services teaching weekly chapel at a local Christian School. He seemed almost perturbed that I had set up those commitments, and wasn't interested in doing either one, although he did accompany me to the soup kitchen a few times.

I acknowledged his leadership and headship in our family and ministry, but I had a right to know what he was doing to help us progress in what we thought God called us to do. So, I asked, but his answers were vague and always defensive. *How dare I question him? If I thought I could do better at making things happen, why didn't I just do it all myself?* You get the idea.

While I've never spoken to my former husband about this at length, it is obvious he was addicted. I've never questioned his love for God, me, or our children. Only an addiction could have led him down the path that destroyed his marriage, family, ministry, and his life. Addicts think they've found relief from the doldrums and pressures of life. Some discover it in food, hording, a bottle, a pill, or through a needle. Others find it through sex. However, addicts soon find that what begins as an enjoyable diversion quickly becomes a cruel slave driver. When they want to stop, they don't know how. They feel helplessly controlled by the addiction's drive.

One writer termed addiction *"a banquet in the grave."* The addict feels as if he is enjoying the best of life; his physical needs are met quickly and in the manner in which he wants them, but the delicacies he partakes of are actually poison. People want addictive substances to serve their needs, but in the end, the addiction enslaves and demands that the addicted individual serve it. No one takes his first drink thinking that one day he won't be able to function without alcohol in his system. Neither does a

---

[1] Welch, Edward T., Addictions - A Banquet in the Grave (Phillipsburg: P&R Publishing, 2001)

person view pornography and believe that the images that seemingly bring so much pleasure will ultimately destroy his or her life.

Most people, including many committed, church-going Christians don't view pornography as a problem. They say things like:

"Is porn really that bad?"
"I keep it private. It doesn't hurt anyone, so what's the problem?"

Pornography is linked to one of the biggest evils in our world today — human trafficking. The International Labour Organization estimates that over 150 million dollars are illegally made through the exploitation of 21 million people, of which 5.5 million are children and 11.4 million are women and girls. One researcher noted a definite connection between porn and prostitution — which feeds the human trafficking industry. She stated, *"Pornography is men's rehearsal for prostitution."*

A high percentage of rescued sex trafficked victims acknowledged that their captors either forced them to perform in pornographic recordings or to watch them as a teaching tool on how to service their *"clients."* Porn is not a *"victimless sin;"* it does hurt people. It will destroy the one watching; it will eventually affect the viewer's personal relationships and physical responses, and thus wound his/her family, and it often hurts nameless faces who are enduring the living hell of sexual slavery that produced it.

Sadly, pornography has become an accepted part of our culture, and whether

---

[2] https://everaccountable.com/blog/the-link-between-pornography-and-human-trafficking/

anyone wants to acknowledge it or not, it has infiltrated the lives of Christians. 53% of the attendees at a national men's ministry conference said they had viewed porn within the past seven days. A 2016 study by Barna Research, funded by Josh McDowell Ministries, revealed that 57% of pastors and 64% of youth pastors admitted to either past or current issues with pornography, although the researchers admitted the numbers might be higher because 55% of the pastors who used porn said they live in constant fear of being found out. 81% of the pastors said they felt *great shame* about their habit. Therefore, it is likely that every pastor queried didn't give a completely honest response. The shame associated with any addiction empowers the addiction and keeps the addicted person from getting help; this is true with any addictive behavior, but a porn addiction is considered the most shameful of all. Porn addiction is kept quiet, especially in the church.

Most people outside of the church consider viewing porn as harmless and normal, and some suggest that married couples should include it in their intimate relationship. To me, that is paramount to saying that instead of sitting down to a lovely prepared meal, you should share the garbage in your trash can with your spouse! Pornography is ubiquitous; it *may* be possible to live your life without ever being exposed to it, but I don't know how. You can't even drive down some of Dallas' major freeways without viewing very suggestive billboards!

Society accepts pornography, but that doesn't mean it's okay, healthy, or normal. Porn is highly addictive, but honestly, everyone who views it will *not* become addicted. They will, however, get twisted ideas about women, sex, and marriage. Pornography creates a false sense of intimacy and attachment. For some women, it leads to anorexia and bulimia as they try to attain the perfect body like the airbrushed versions online. Men will likely buy into the image that sex is all about their ultimate pleasure, and whatever it takes to get there is what their wife should do. Sex, for the porn viewer, becomes about performance and pleasure. God created sex for pleasure, but He intends it to be an expression of love between a husband and wife, not a selfish indulgence for personal gratification. Porn will weaken your intimate relationship with your spouse; it will not enhance it.

While everyone who views porn will not become an addict, many people are inclined to addictive behaviors, and porn is an easy addiction to acquire. You don't have to meet a dealer on a street corner or sneak bottles in from the liquor store. All you have to do is turn on your computer and connect to the Internet. An individual with a family background of addictive behavior may be more prone, but anyone who has an unmet emotional need is a candidate for some type of addiction — alcohol, drugs, and sex are the top three. With porn, you don't have to swallow, inhale, or inject anything to get a euphoric high — the videos or pictures arouse you, and the "feel good" hormones flow freely!

Many studies today claim that an addiction to porn is harder to break than an addiction to cocaine. Sexual addiction is progressive. In other words, what excited an individual at first ceases to do the trick, and he/she seeks out more graphic and explicit content. For my former spouse, it led to interacting with teenage girls online.

The four stages of pornography addiction are listed by Gene McConnell and Keith Campbell in an article posted on the *Focus on the Family* website. They are:

1. Early exposure. Most guys who get addicted to porn start early. They see stuff when they are very young, and it gets its foot in the door.

2. Escalation. After a while, escalation begins. You start to look for more and more graphic porn. You start using porn that you would have been disgusted with when you started. Now it excites you.

3. Desensitization. Eventually, you start to become numb. Even the most graphic, degrading porn doesn't excite you anymore. You become desperate to feel the same thrill again but can't find it.

4. Acting out sexually. At this point, many men make a dangerous jump and start acting out sexually. They move from the paper and plastic image of porn to the real world.

The fourth stage of pornography addiction cannot be overlooked. Since much porn depicts men as aggressors and women as their willing victims, when the *acting out sexually* stage sets in, it often leads to criminal activity.

Ted Bundy is perhaps the most notorious rapist and serial killer of the modern era. Between 1974-1978, he admitted to the rape and murder of 30 young women, although authorities are sure the count was much

---

[3] https://focusonthefamily.com/marriage/divorce-and-infidelity/pornography-and-virtual-infidelity/stages-of-porn-addiction

higher. He was 42 years old when he was put to death in the electric chair in a Florida prison. On the night before he died, he allowed James Dobson, a minister and founder of *Focus on the Family*, to interview him. He acknowledged that the rapes and murders he committed were the manifestations of the fourth stage of his long-held porn addiction.

Like most other kinds of addiction, I would keep looking for more potent, more explicit, more graphic types of material. Like an addiction, you keep craving something which is hard, harder, something which gives you a greater sense of excitement. Until you reach the point that pornography only goes so far. I've lived in prison a long time now. I've met a lot of men who were motivated to commit violence just like me. And without exception, every one of them was deeply involved in pornography. Without question, without exception, deeply influenced and consumed by addiction to pornography.[sic] [4]

Of course, most people don't start in the fourth stage. They begin with *early exposure*. My former husband was introduced to porn as an adolescent, and his arrest and conviction prove that he walked through all four stages.

I've wrestled with the fact that he was trapped in an FBI sting. We received conflicting reports, and even today, there are differing facts online about whether he ever sent or requested lewd pictures to/with an actual underage girl or if all of the transmissions were between him and

---

[4] https://www.1.cbn.com/cbnnews/us/2018/october/serial-killer-ted-bundy-describes-the-dangers-of-pornography

an agent *claiming* to be a 15 or 16-year-old girl. Regardless, he acted out by sending and requesting lewd pictures, and I am thankful that was as far as it got. Had he not been caught in the FBI sting, who knows what his fantasies might have driven him to do if the addiction was allowed to progress?

He confessed to me after his arrest that the escalation of his addiction began when, as a young man, he would be aroused by seeing a photo of a woman in a tight sweater, but soon that wasn't enough. This was long before the Internet, but pornographic magazines and paperback novels were plenteous even in those days, and porn became part of his life. It only made sense that he would introduce his young and extremely naïve bride to his hitherto private indulgence. His intentions might have been good. He may have wanted to be open and honest; he may have assumed it would increase my desire or response. It was a whole new world for me! I had never seen it, but I assumed that since my husband initiated it, and as long as another person wasn't physically involved in the act of marriage, it was okay. Thankfully, a dear Christian friend of ours told us that porn is *not* an acceptable part of the marriage bed! Perhaps it's too strong to say that I *forced* him to throw it all out, but I made it clear that we wouldn't have it in our home.

He has told me (and I believe him) that there were periods through our 30-year marriage when he stayed clean, but when life got the most stressful, he resorted to his old ways. Only once, after we threw the magazines out of our house (within our first year of marriage) did I ever catch him looking at something inappropriate online. It was several years before we went into the ministry, but we were plugged into an excellent church. I knew better by then about God's expectations for appropriate sexual gratification, and I assumed he did too. When I saw the picture on the computer screen, I got heated. I don't remember all the details, but I do remember that I said, *"That is nothing but an open door to the devil. I will NOT have my children put at risk by allowing this in our house!"* I wasn't exactly soft-spoken about it.

He promised me it was a mistake. It just *popped up; he had no idea where it came from! He didn't do that anymore.* Once I took such a firm stand against it, he knew from then on, if he were going to partake of porn, he would have to hide it from me. I assumed the issue was finished. I was wrong. He simply got better at hiding it.

*And he said unto me,
My grace is sufficient for thee:
for my strength is made perfect in weakness.
Most gladly therefore will I rather
glory in my infirmities, that the power
of Christ may rest
upon me.*

2 Corinthians 12:9 | KJV

CHAPTER 13
Why Did God Let This Happen?

When the rug was pulled out from under my life, I got a little shaky; I cried and screamed a little, lost a lot of weight (not entirely a bad thing), but I never doubted God for a moment. However, many, if not most people who believe in God and know that He is all-powerful often encounter a crisis of faith when *stuff happens,* and life deals them a bad hand.

When the doctor's diagnosis is *terminal,* when the loved one dies long before they've achieved old age, when natural disasters destroy cities and homes and lives, and when innocent children or women are emotionally or physically abused or hurt, they want to know *why.*

"Why did God let it happen?"

"Isn't He loving?"

"Isn't He all-powerful?"

"Doesn't He care?"

People going through painful situations often conclude that God must not exist. If He did, He *never* would have allowed the tragedy to take place. After all, if He is love, the way the Bible describes Him, He would have supernaturally intervened to stop it, wouldn't He?

The answer to that rhetorical question is "No."

Let me try to explain without going into too much Biblical doctrine. Every engaging novel has good guys and bad guys — forces of righteousness and of forces of evil, but somehow people forget that the fundamental storyline of good vs. evil is founded on reality. God is good. He is a Spirit, and we can't usually see Him. However, God has an antithesis on this earth. In the Old Testament, he's called Lucifer, but the New Testament calls him the devil or Satan. He is bad. He too is a spirit, and we can't usually see him, but he is alive and well and influencing activity all over the world. In my case, he was working in the basement of our home!

The Bible calls Satan the *god of this world (2 Corinthians 4:4)*. He is not all-powerful like God, but he does have power. He is not all-knowing like God, but he is very observant. He knows what bait every individual is most likely to take. In my former husband's case, the bait was sexual gratification.

Jesus said that Satan comes to *steal, kill, and destroy (John 10:10)*. God is all good; the devil is all evil. He is a liar. He tempts people with their weakness and then assures them that *"It will be okay. No one will get hurt. You'll never get caught. God wants you to enjoy life, right?"*

Sin always feels good for a time; otherwise, why would people do it? However, the sweet taste of pleasure soon turns into the bitterness of regret. The Bible says that *the wages of sin are death (Romans 6:23)*. Death may be physical, emotional, or spiritual. God is against sin because sin pays up — not always every two weeks like your job, but it always pays in pain. Bodies break down, families are destroyed, and finances, careers, and ministries are ruined by sin.

The logical question arises, *"If God is all-powerful, why doesn't He just get rid of the devil? Why do we have to deal with evil, pain, sickness, hurt, and loss? Can't God do it?"* God *could,* but He *won't* because He can do anything *except* violate His promises. God created man to be like Himself — with self-determination and will, and He promised to give humans authority on the earth.

And God said, Let us make man in our image, after our likeness: and let them have dominion over the fish of the sea, and over the fowl of the air, and over the cattle, and over all the earth, and over every creeping thing that creepeth upon the earth. (Genesis 1:26)

When God gave authority to Adam and Eve, He vowed not to run this world as a puppet master. God never forces His will on anyone. He created Adam and Eve as free moral agents. He could have forced them to obey, but He didn't. He placed one tree out of possibly thousands in the Garden of Eden from which they were not to eat. God gave them free choice and free will. They chose to disobey, and they reaped precisely what God told them they would.

And the LORD God commanded the man, saying, Of every tree of the garden thou mayest freely eat: But of the tree of the knowledge of good and evil, thou shalt not eat of it: for in the day that thou eatest thereof thou shalt surely die. (Genesis 2:16-17)

The same is true today. God does not force anyone to do what is good, right, moral, or just. Everyone has free choice and free will. Like Adam and Eve, they can choose to do good — God's will, or they can choose to do evil — the devil's will.

The man who went by the title of *pastor,* and who was married to me for nearly 31 years, had a choice, and he repeatedly made the wrong one. God is so kind and merciful that He will try to get your attention. If you are cruising down a road that leads to destruction, God will send signs, people and maybe even blinking lights to get your attention, but you still have to observe those warnings, acknowledge you're heading the wrong way, and turn around!

Shortly after I moved to Austin, my eyes were opened, and I became aware of God's attempt to stop the destruction we went through in Lubbock — and even before we were married. We had three odd interactions with people in Lubbock that I now know were God's messengers of warning.

The first was impersonal but very clear in my memory. Just a few weeks after we moved to Lubbock, the local news carried a story about a pastor of a small church who was charged with molesting a young woman. I remember seeing his mugshot on the news. The report said that he was married and had a few children. I clearly recall feeling sick for the wife and children. In researching for this book, I learned that he maintained his innocence and, after a jury trial that ended in a hung jury (favoring his innocence), the charges were eventually dropped several years later. I don't know him or his family, but I am certain that the charges cost him dearly financially, emotionally, and professionally.

The second was more up close and personal. An elderly couple who attended our church for several weeks requested prayer and help for their adult son, who was in his 40s — very close to our ages at the time. He was about to be released from prison. Can you take a wild guess at why he was in jail? I don't remember the exact charges against him, but it had to do with underage sexual contact and pornography. I recall talking to my husband about them. How horrible for them to watch their son have to go to prison, and now he couldn't find a job or a place to live because he was a registered sex offender.

The third warning was cryptic, and to this day, I'm not sure, but I think the FBI might have approached a gentleman who attended our church. He was a wrestling coach at Texas Tech, an incredibly sharp man, and as I recall he was single. He helped us paint the new building, and was always willing to pitch in. He called to set up a meeting with us one day. We assumed he had a personal or spiritual issue he wanted to discuss. However, just before we met, we got another phone call from him. He made some ambiguous statement about not being able to talk to us, and that was the last we saw of him.

God was trying to stop the destruction. He sent messages and messengers, but if we refuse to listen, He won't force His will. He will allow us to self-destruct.

I believe God tried to protect me even before we married. To say that I was naïve at that time would be an understatement. I was in college and hadn't seriously dated anyone for several years. Then I met a guy who gave me a lot of attention. He was the paid star of several of the Lyric Opera productions I performed in as a Music Theater major. He was more forward sexually than I was accustomed to, but I figured it was okay because we were getting serious and after all, he was a star, and I was in the chorus.

I knew very little about the Bible and Christianity. I was just a Catholic girl who loved Jesus. I never heard about Paul's warning not to marry an unbeliever: *Be ye not unequally yoked together with unbelievers: for what fellowship hath righteousness with unrighteousness? and what communion hath light with darkness? (2 Corinthians 6:14)* When Dean asked me to marry him, I didn't have a sense of peace, but I felt like we had gone too far in our relationship for me to back out. Honestly, I felt like marrying him would make everything right, and it would all work out in the end.

I was attending the Catholic Charismatic prayer group on the campus of Arizona State University fairly regularly. Although we met at the Newman Center (the Catholic community on campus), everyone who attended was not a student. I'll never forget the red-headed flamboyant Italian grandmother who blessed us all with boxes of home-made cookies on a regular basis. She loved God, and I believe she was a woman of prayer. As part of the Charismatic group, she often had what we called a *Word from the Lord*. Some Christians use other terms like *prophecy, word of wisdom, or word of knowledge*.

Like many people who hear clearly from God, she was a little odd. She spoke with a heavy accent, and well, she was old. I was 21. More than once, she confronted me about marrying my fiancé. *"Why are you marrying him?"* I dismissed her question as the nosey interrogation of an old lady. Another time she got bolder, "Look at him. He's bald. You can do better than that. Why are you marrying him?" I can still see her head with unkempt and curly red hair. She had to look up at me — and I'm only 5'2", but she was as serious as a heart attack. She did not want me to go through with the wedding.

I don't know if she knew that I was marrying an unbeliever or not. The pastor, a priest, however, was well aware. I went to him before we even got engaged because, when I asked Dean about his religion, he told me that he was a Christian Scientist.

At first, I didn't have any concerns; all I heard was *Christian.* Then I did some research and learned that Christian Scientists don't believe in sin (or a personal devil or hell), and they don't believe in the atoning death of Jesus Christ or His resurrection. They believe that all matter is an illusion, and all sickness is nothing more than *"error of the mind."* When I realized what his beliefs were, I ran to my parish priest to ask him if I should break it off with this guy because we got serious pretty quickly. Knowing what I know now, the priest's answer shocks me. But then, as an infatuated and already overly committed 21-year-old girl, I was grateful for it.

"Well, Gloria, if he were Mormon, I'd say you should break it off for sure. But Christian Science is different. They don't really proselytize. As a matter of fact, my mother died several years ago, and my father recently remarried a Christian Scientist, and they seem to be quite happy."

So, on June 30, 1979, we got married, and I started praying like only a wife can for her husband to come to know Jesus. I introduced him to friends who also prayed for and reached out to him. Just before our first wedding anniversary, he went out of town to attend a special yearly Christian Science meeting. I stayed home and prayed. When he came back from that meeting, he told me that he knew that Christian Science was wrong. He had met Jesus through my friends and me, and he wanted the real deal. I thank God that, regardless of what happened almost 30 years later, that man will make his eternal home in heaven, and so will our children and grandchildren.

I don't blame God for the crisis I went through. God tried to warn me, but God's great mercy triumphed despite my ignorance and/or disobedience. He loved me despite it all, and He never, ever left me!

CHAPTER 14
Awkward Moments

If there's one thing my mother taught me, it was to be polite. Say *please* and *thank you;* engage in polite conversation, and for heaven's sake, don't bring up anything inappropriate. Don't initiate conversation about possibly embarrassing or awkward topics. Stick with safe things — the weather, fashion, music, and maybe sports. I think most people were taught the same kind of manners, which makes it quite awkward for people to interact with someone whose family name has just been smeared like manure all over the Internet.

It was hard for me, too. What do I tell whom? Should I ask what they know or simply assume that they've heard? How much do they need to know, anyway?

A few days after the FBI walked into my house unannounced, I got a phone call from a pastor that I had preached for several times. I respected what he and his wife were doing in their community, and they were always gracious. They let me bring whatever Word the Lord gave me to minister, and their congregation received it with beautiful, open hearts. The Holy Spirit was allowed to do His thing in that church, and I loved ministering there.

He called on the worst possible day, and as I recall, the worst possible time of the day. I had just gotten off the phone with administrative people who worked for my pastor. They had given me a list of things I needed to do to close up church business in Lubbock. I didn't ask, but I assume they couldn't work through Dean because they needed to distance themselves from him completely, but either way, I was serving as co-pastor, so it wasn't totally unexpected that I would be called upon to close things up.

I don't remember whether or not my phone recognized the pastor's number. I don't think it did, and I was surprised when I heard his voice. He called to let me know about his church's upcoming anniversary celebration and a special offering they were receiving for it.

I was breathless and panicked. Sadly, I didn't think about his church, which I loved, or he and his wife and their kindness towards me over the past several years. My mind started racing. *Obviously, he doesn't know yet. It only happened yesterday, and the news hasn't gotten out yet. Do I tell him? What do I say? I don't even know what to say except that the FBI walked into my house a few days ago and it looks like they're going to arrest my husband.*

If he were to call me today, I would say, *"Oh, pastor! Congratulations! We would be honored to send an offering to bless you and your church family!"* However, on December 17, 2009, I said something more like, *"Uh..., I'm so sorry...but...um...you caught me at a bad time."* It was awkward, and he probably thought I was horribly rude and uncaring! I still wince when I remember that conversation.

As I mentioned earlier, in Lubbock, I was on the *buy-one-get-one-free* plan that most ministerial spouses enjoy. In other words, we both did the work; I actually preached much more than he did, probably about 85% of the time, but only my husband was paid, so I still did a little bit of itinerant preaching as well. When I officially went on staff in Round

Rock, one of the stipulations of being a ministerial employee was that we were not permitted to pursue our own ministry. So, I stopped contacting the pastors who had me in to preach. Unfortunately, over the years, I lost track of this pastor. I tried to call him to tell him why my response sounded so selfish and rude, but I couldn't find his contact information anywhere. Perhaps somehow, he will get a copy of this book and understand my awkward and seemingly self-centered response!

Ebeth's high school graduation was another opportunity for awkward moments. She graduated from Round Rock Christian School, but since she was only there for a little over four months, and was working part-time, few even knew who she was except some people who worked in administration. Her official graduation would be there, but her school in Lubbock was where she had spent the last year. The parents and kids knew her. She led worship in their weekly chapel services and sang the National Anthem at basketball games. She had some good, close friends there although she had only been there one year.

Our pastor friends, who oversee the school in Lubbock were tremendously kind to allow her to walk with her class. They generously paid for a hotel for us in Lubbock. They understood the financial mess I had assumed and knew that a hotel was not in my budget. My son traveled from California to Lubbock so he could watch his little sister walk across the stage with people who at least knew her. Our pastor friends spent some time with us and took the kids and me out to lunch. Their kindness and consideration will always live in my memory, and I believe God will bless them for the seed they sowed into my family.

Part of the graduation celebration included the presentation of the graduate's life and accomplishments. Each grad was assigned a table in the church's fellowship hall. The parents created displays with pictures, awards, and memorabilia about their child's life up through 12th grade. Some brought in trophies, ribbons, and other things to show off what their child had accomplished. Some of these tables looked like they belonged on HGTV. They were gorgeous. I tried to represent my wonderful daughter well but display and décor are not my strong suits.

Parents, teachers, relatives, students, and the graduates mingled from table to table, admiring each other's achievements. It was lovely, but for my family, it was terribly awkward. Very few people came by to look at Ebeth's table, and those who did didn't have much to say. I don't blame anyone in the least, and I wasn't offended. I understood. First of all, her father was there, and his face had been splattered all over the local news for the last four months as an accused sex offender. Who wants to come to interact with that? Second, what would they say? Every interaction for me was awkward. We tried hard to act like we were a nice, normal family with a wonderful daughter graduating from a highly respected Christian school, but everyone knew differently.

The next week I got to repeat the graduate presentation program in Round Rock. It was easier for me because her dad wasn't there, but she was almost a total stranger to the students, parents, and teachers at that school. Again, we didn't have much traffic at our table; I don't know if it affected her or not. Thankfully, her youth pastors came and so did some of our Round Rock family. I didn't ask her if she felt bad because no one at the school knew her very well. We just did the best we could and carried on regardless of how we felt. I always taught her that feelings lie anyway! God's Word is the truth, and God's Word says He had a hope and a future for her and for me *(Jeremiah 29:11)*.

*For I know
the plans I have for you,
says the Lord.
They are plans for good
and not for disaster, to give you
a future and
a hope.*

Jeremiah 29:11 | NLT

CHAPTER 15
Help

Knowing that life's crises create awkward moments for friends and acquaintances, I tried to be understanding about the fact that when people suffer, others who want to help don't always know how to respond. I am sure that a lot of people were praying for us, but I heard from very few. After all, what is the right thing to do to help someone who encounters a life-altering incident? Do you reach out or give them their space? Should you take a casserole or simply pray? It all depends. However, one thing you shouldn't do is try to get information about the gory details — especially if you are no more than a casual acquaintance.

Only a day or two after the crisis hit, I got a text from an unknown phone number. The text said something to the effect of, *"I heard the news. Is it true?"* The number was from Phoenix, where I had lived for 30 years, but I had no idea who it was. I replied with the obvious question, *"Who is this?"* The person told me he knew us from our church in Phoenix. Okay. So, now I'm wondering how fast and far the news had spread! This was someone with whom I had absolutely no interaction. He wasn't part of our small group, Bible Study, or neighborhood. How in the world did he hear about our crisis? Suddenly I envisioned a great screen covering America and broadcasting the news of my family's personal downfall. I pictured some spreading the word and enjoying the show, and it hurt. As politely, but as honestly as I could, I replied, *"I hope that you are praying for us and not talking about us."* He assured me he was, and I chose to believe him.

My pastor knew what to do to help. He stepped in and assisted my daughter and me in more ways than I can count. First of all, he graciously created a job for me. Had he not done that my life today would be completely different.

Second, he kept in contact with me. He lived in Michigan and only came to Lubbock to fire my former husband and close our church. He or his wife wasn't around to visit or help us in person. He did, however, call me regularly until my daughter and I got out of Lubbock. The conversations were always short. Like most preachers, he is a man of few words — except when he's in the pulpit. He would ask how I was, how my daughter was, and sometimes he would explain legal proceedings or things I needed to do to close up the business aspect of the church before I left for Austin. He helped us financially by handing my husband's severance pay over to me.

After we moved to Austin, my pastor met with me on a fairly regular basis to see how I was doing and what was happening. I didn't have any long, drawn-out counseling sessions, but they were frequent. He counsels by the Word of God. He didn't encourage me to relive the shock, hurt, and pain, or to verbalize the negatives. He focused my attention on God, His Word, and what Jesus had already done for me. Most of our visits were very short and unemotional. I knew what to do. I knew how to get through a crisis by speaking the Word of God. I understood the power of gratitude, and I challenged myself whenever I was in an emotional funk to verbally thank God for everything — and I mean *everything*. I specifically remember one morning when I was exhausted and was dealing with several issues on the legal front. I wanted to be depressed. I thought I deserved sympathy, but I knew that even the best sympathy in the world wouldn't help me. So, I began to thank God for every little thing I could think of.

"Thank you, God, for my feet."

"Thank you that I can walk and talk and see and chew food!"

"Thank you for my shoes."

"Thank you for my ears."

"Thank you for my earrings."

I realized that, as bad as my situation was, there were women in the world who had things worse than I. I had a job and a roof over my head. I had two great adult children who loved God, each other, and their mother! I had a pastor who cared for me and about me. I didn't need much counseling because I knew the power of praise and thanksgiving. I had taught it for years in Bible Schools and from pulpits; I was simply practicing what I preached.

My pastor wanted to assure that my daughter and I would be safe now that we were living as single women. He trained us both on how to use a firearm. Neither one of us had ever handled a gun. We were both a bit skittish, but he was a superb teacher. He made sure we knew the safety rules before he would let us touch a gun. He taught us how to handle the weapon correctly and even how to clean it and care for it. He made sure I got to the range regularly so my skills would stay sharp. He taught me how to clear my house and had me practice what to do if an intruder came in. He made sure that I placed night lights throughout our home in

Round Rock so that if a security issue happened, we could find our way to safety. He taught us how to live our lives on "yellow," staying aware of our surroundings, looking for the closest exit in every building, and keeping our heads on a swivel.

My pastor has trained many people to shoot, and I'm sure I wasn't the best shot he'd ever trained; I may have been one of the worst. He couldn't figure out why my aim was so poor, and neither could I. I was sure trying! Eventually, we discovered that I am left-eye dominant, and I was using my right eye. Once we got that figured out, we were both a lot less frustrated! He got me to an LTC (License to Carry) class after he knew I could pass the range exam, and I passed! Training this *suddenly single* woman and her daughter to protect themselves was a huge blessing in our lives. I still enjoy going to the range, and I just renewed my Texas LTC.

My sister knew what to do to help, as well. Jennifer lives in Columbus, Ohio, but after we moved to Austin, she flew out to be with us. My garage was packed with boxes — most of which were full of my former husband's things. He had already been sentenced to 10 years, and Federal law required he serve 85% of the sentence, so he was gone for at least 8 ½ years. I didn't know what to do with all of his stuff. Although we were divorced, I hadn't yet made the complete emotional break, and I wanted to hold onto whatever I could. I had several large wardrobe boxes of his clothes and shoes. My thought was, *"He's going to need clothes when he gets out."* I was either planning on dragging those boxes around with me for the next decade, or I was going to ask my dear Round Rock friends to keep them in their storage unit for him. Thankfully, my sister brought me to my senses. *"Gloria, really, he's going to be gone for almost ten years.*

Moths will eat these, or they won't be in style anyway by then. Let them go. You can buy him new clothes."

She helped me sort out memorabilia, pictures, and yearbooks. We put some in a box for my kids. Their memories of their dad were still important. However, we threw out his high school yearbooks and held a garage sale to get rid of opera scores, music resources, and tools that I didn't even know how to use. I felt lighter after the garage was cleaned. When she went back to Ohio, she called me every day for about six months. Sometimes I would have a lot to say; other times I didn't, but every time she called it reminded me that I was not alone and that we would get through this. Her visit brought her and Ebeth, her niece, closer than I ever would have imagined. They both developed a great respect for each other that is still intact today. Jennifer often mailed us coupons or gift cards to Steak and Shake because she learned on one of our phone calls that Ebeth and I went to Steak and Shake every Thursday after our midweek church service and treated ourselves to half-price milkshakes! We were on such a tight budget. Our days were brighter when I got an envelope in the mail from my dear sister in Columbus, Ohio!

My money situation was dire. I took on tens of thousands of dollars of debt, most of which I didn't know about before December 14. Thankfully, some debt didn't have my name or signature, and I realized that I wouldn't be held responsible for that. I discovered how to check my credit and how to get items removed that weren't legally mine. It took some work, but it was worth it. However, the debt that did have my name on it was sizeable, and my starting salary in Austin was that of a first-year minister.

The financial pressure was severe, but I trusted God, kept paying my tithe, and continued to pray. One morning I woke up with an idea that I believe was from the Holy Spirit. I sent an email to close friends and family who had expressed concern or asked what they could do to help us. I told them as honestly and graciously as I could, *"We need money."* I didn't say it quite that bluntly, but I let them know how, if they so desired, they could give to us. I also let them know that I still had an Amway business and that if they ordered products on my website, it would help us pay our bills.

Some of my dear friends began to give generously every month to help us. One of my brothers sent me a sizeable check. Others bought products from my website, and I began to dig myself out of debt. Three years later, I had brought about $40,000 in debt down to about $15,000, but that last debt was on a very high interest revolving credit card. The interest alone was $250 a month. I felt like I was digging myself out of quicksand; the more I dug, the more I sunk. Thankfully, my big-hearted father blessed me with a brand-new Nissan Altima. I thank God for my dad's generosity and sensitivity to my needs. I never told him that the car I was driving had the "check engine" light on and wouldn't pass the Texas vehicle requirements for license renewal, but somehow, he just knew what I needed and when I needed it. I still drive that car today and fondly remember my dad, who now lives in heaven.

Three years after acquiring my new wheels, I finally got the idea to take a low-interest rate loan out on that car. It was enough to pay off the exorbitantly high-interest credit card, and a few years later, I paid off the loan on the car and wiped out all of the debt. I could tangibly sense the power of people's prayers for me as I dug myself out of my financial and emotional mess, and I was grateful. However, I was extremely thankful that some people did more than pray. The truth be told, some Christians use prayer as an easy out for rendering aid to those in need.

If you know someone whose life has been suddenly upended by a crisis, you should definitely pray for them, but don't stop there. I can almost guarantee that unless they are extremely wealthy, they need money. Don't be concerned about offending them by sending them some cash or a gift card. Don't ask if they need money; they do. Just send some. You also might call them periodically and see how they're doing. Don't pry; don't ask too many questions. Allow the person to talk as much or as little as they wish, but it's good to discuss some *normal* things that aren't related to the crisis. *What are you cooking for dinner? Have you begun binge-watching a new series on Netflix or Amazon Prime?* Remind your friend that life still holds many enjoyable experiences. The sad and the bad that they experienced was real, but so is the joyful and the good that lies ahead.

Trust in the Lord
with all thine heart; and lean not
unto thine own understanding.
In all thy ways acknowledge him,
and he shall direct
thy paths.

Proverbs 3:5-6 | KJV

CHAPTER 16
Another Move

Two years after Ebeth and I moved to Round Rock, it was time for me to relocate again. My pastor had opened a church in Dallas in 2011. I had been traveling back and forth, assisting him in getting it off the ground. By early 2012, he needed me in Dallas full-time. I wasn't relishing the idea of moving again, particularly since this move would be completely solo. Ebeth was staying in Round Rock where she was on staff as the Youth Minister; she also was traveling to other of my pastor's churches leading worship, and he wanted her to stay put for the time being. My girl had to grow up fast. She didn't get to go to college and enjoy late nights eating pizza with the girls in the dorm. At 19 years old, she found her own apartment, eventually got a roommate, and started paying all of her own bills.

I made two trips to Dallas to find a place to live. I insisted on finding a place to rent that was close to the church. The Dallas-Fort Worth Metroplex is enormous — and when I say huge — I mean in Texas terms! It encompasses 9,286 square miles making it bigger than the states of Rhode Island and Connecticut put together! The 6.8 million people have plenty of room per person — until they make their commutes to and from work.

I would be the Senior Assistant Pastor in Dallas, as I was in Round Rock, which meant that I would be on call 24/7. I didn't want to get stuck in traffic if the ministry needed me on-site in a hurry. I also knew that the stress of commuting wouldn't be healthy for me. My friend from Round

Rock accompanied me on my first attempt in finding a place to live. We didn't find anything workable for me. Everything was either too expensive, too far, or too dilapidated. We did, however, notice the most well-kept little house across the street from one that didn't make the cut. It was only about 5 miles from the church, and I wouldn't even have to take a freeway to work! My friend said, *"That house is so cute. Too bad it isn't for rent."* I agreed and gave up the search for at least another week.

I never enjoyed moving, especially when I didn't have money to walk into a city and just buy a house! We had made a significant move about every 30 months since Dean and I began in full-time ministry. I learned long ago that the housing in the new city was never as nice and never as inexpensive as you see online. Every move required faith for housing. During one of my moves, I found a Scripture to stand on. *Acts 17:25* from my old NIV Bible reads: *[God] made every nation of men, that they should inhabit the whole earth; and He determined the times set for them and the exact places where they should live.* I began to declare that God knew the exact location where I should live in Dallas, and I wouldn't worry about it.

The next weekend, I just happened to drive by that cute little house that was so close to the church, and I saw a small, nearly illegible sign in the yard. It was for rent, and it was a perfect home for a single woman — a 2-bedroom, 1-bath totally updated bungalow from the 1940s. It had a gas fireplace and a lovely deck in the back with a large and peaceful yard. It was a little above what I want to pay, but every move seemed to require me to pony up more in rent money than I wanted. The landlords were sweet, and they worked with me, giving me a slight break on rent.

They knew I'd be a good tenant with no wild parties, and who would care for the place.

I sold much of the big furniture that I had brought from Lubbock to Round Rock. The Dallas house was too small for most of it, and anyway, it was time to part with the huge king size bed and the leather furniture my former husband had hand-picked. A few family heirlooms went to an Austin Auction house, and they helped pay some of my relocation expenses that weren't covered by my employer. For the third time in as many years, I started packing up my every earthly belonging.

My position at the Dallas church was a blessing. I learned, grew, and was challenged. But work was all I had there. I had lost some weight before I moved to Dallas, but after I didn't have a daughter to think about feeding, I really began to shed the pounds. I didn't see any point in cooking for myself. I ate a salad every night for dinner, and I usually worked through lunch. I ate an apple or some trail mix throughout the day to keep me going, but I rarely went to lunch. Pretty soon, all of my clothes were literally hanging off of my body. My pastor's wife ran into me one day at a store in Dallas, and when I tried on some pants, I asked her if they were too tight. She kindly, but honestly told me, *"No, Gloria. That is the way pants are supposed to fit."*

I was grateful that I usually got to see my daughter at least once a week. She was serving as the Youth Pastor in both Round Rock and Dallas for a while. She traveled to Dallas on Wednesday for a staff meeting and youth service, but we didn't have much time to enjoy one another. She also came to Dallas once or twice a month to lead praise and worship on Sundays.

Those weekends were precious to me. We found our favorite Mexican restaurants in my new digs and charted out the best places to shop. We continued to laugh at the oddities of our life. My daughter had become my friend — a friend I highly respected. She was the one who, when I wanted to sob, would find something fun for us to do. She would tell me to get dressed up, put on some make-up, and get me out of the house. She would play Super Chick music as loud as my old ears could stand it and we would rock out to their fantastic woman-empowering faith-filled songs!

She had weathered the same storm I had, but as a teenager. Now she was my co-laborer in Christ.

CHAPTER 17
Online

As much as I enjoyed my daughter's visits to Dallas, we were told they would be winding down, and she would be serving exclusively in Round Rock. A few months later, I found myself sitting on my living room sofa on a Sunday night. I had worked long hours that day, but I still wanted to be able to go to dinner, watch a movie, or just laugh with someone. My house was quiet, and I was lonely.

I didn't envision my life in Dallas like this. I thought I would have some kind of social life. Although I hadn't begun dating anyone, both of my kids had talked to me about it. Periodically, when Ebeth would help me update my make-up and my clothing style, she would say something like, *"Don't dress like an old lady."* What she meant was, *"If you're going to find a man, you can't be looking like a granny!"*

I lived in a very trendy part of the city close to Love Field. I took myself out to dinner at least once a week, and I fully expected some fine, wealthy cowboy to notice me. After all, I had an updated wardrobe. I was down to a size 2, and I looked okay for a 50+-year-old lady! Obviously, I didn't hang out in bars, but truthfully, I thought someone would find me at the local farm-to-market restaurant that I frequented! I tried to look available, but not easy.

Hello? See? I'm single. I don't have on a ring. I'm sitting by myself. Hello?

I had a grand total of zero men approach me. Zero. None. At all.

My pastor had told me several months back that he knew I wasn't meant to live the rest of my life as a single woman; I was meant to be someone's wife. I agreed. I knew it in my spirit, but dear Lord! I wasn't in my 30s. I wanted to be married while we could still enjoy…married stuff. Where was this man? Wherever he was, he didn't seem to frequent the same restaurants or grocery stores I did!

So, on that Sunday night in July 2012, I talked with the Lord.

"Lord, what's up? Here I am, serving you, but I have no personal life at all! You didn't create me to live like this. What am I supposed to do?"

He answered me.

"Get on your iPad and find a Christian dating site."

"But Lord," I protested. *"My pastor is against those. One of my employees even said from the pulpit at a women's meeting that Christian women don't go to dating websites."*

God is good. He is honest and understandable too.

"Is your pastor here with you tonight? No, he is at home with his wife. You will answer to Me in the end, not him. Just trust Me."

So, I did what the Holy Spirit told me to do. I searched on my iPad for Christian dating sites. Three popped up. Two of them do a lot of advertising, and I was familiar with their names. The third was more obscure. I had never seen an ad for it, nor had I heard anyone mention it in conversation. That was the one I felt led to visit. I filled out a profile and started my 7-day free trial on *Christian Cafe* website on July 15, 2012.

Later, I discovered that this site is the only one of the three that was founded and owned by Christians. The other "Christian singles" sites merely marketed to Christians. The site Holy Spirit led me to was very particular about what was posted, and they approve all pictures before they're published on the site.

I didn't download a photo that night. To this day, I'm not terribly techy, but in 2012, I was even less techy. I usually called on my kids when I needed pictures downloaded from one place to another, but I didn't want to tell them I was on a Christian singles' website. After all, they knew our pastor looked down on such things. What would they think?

The questions in the members' profiles asked each person to reveal various pieces of information. For example, where they were from, what they do for a living, and what they were interested in. While I joined a *Christian dating site,* I don't believe in going online to get a date; that attitude can lead to risky interactions. I wasn't looking for a different guy to take me out to dinner every week. I was looking for a strong Christian husband, and I was honest about it. The profile asked each member what kind of relationship they were looking for — short term, long term, or marriage. I wanted to be married.

I answered the questions on the profile honestly, but as simply as I could. Thankfully, the website made the picture download process reasonably easy, and I was determined to figure it out. I had to crop Ebeth out of the photo I was posting, so it took me a little longer. I posted a decent and fun black and white picture that Ebeth and I took together on one of her recent visits to Dallas. As soon as my picture went up, I started getting inquiries. Yes, men are visual creatures.

The profile asked questions about age; it offered ranges, so I didn't have to reveal my exact age. It also asked if I was looking for someone older, younger, or the same age. Knowing that older men often want younger women, I figured that the ones who would be interested in me would likely be in their 80s. So, I specified on my profile that I was looking for someone a little younger than me because I wrote, *"I am younger than my age."* I hoped it would discourage the 80 and 90-year-olds from contacting me. I didn't, however, expect the opposite. A dear young man, in his 30s, saw my request for a younger man as an invitation. As flattering as that was, I had to tell him (more than once) that while I wanted someone younger than me, I would not consider dating anyone who was the same age as my son!

My profile revealed my profession, and since this was an openly Christian site, I wasn't surprised that I got some responses from men in ministry who wrote to me about going all over the world and preaching the Gospel with them. The approach should have interested me, but they didn't seem authentic. I wasn't looking for a preaching partner. I was looking for a husband.

I responded kindly and politely to every inquiry, but none of them caught my attention until Thursday, July 19. It was my day off, and I had several errands to run. I was going to the gym, getting the oil changed, and I also had a technician coming to the house to install a burglar alarm — at my pastor's insistence. (He wasn't happy when he found out I hadn't initiated service on my security system.)

While I waited for the representative to arrive for his appointment, I got a notification from *Christian Cafe*. Someone had sent me a message or had "winked" at me. I never responded to "winks," which are akin to "nudges" or "waves" on Facebook. As far as I was concerned, if someone was interested in me, then they should have the courtesy to say something to me, not merely "wink" at me!

When I logged in, I saw that it wasn't a "wink," so I opened it and read a short, but perfectly written note.

Okay, you are gorgeous, accomplished, articulate, focused and all that good stuff. What the heck are you doing here?

Oh, and I may be 52, which is outside your prescribed age parameters per your description, but in all fairness, "you ain't the only one younger than your age."

Now that the prerequisite nonsense is out of the way, Howya doin'?

Mike

He got my attention. What woman would reject a message like that? He seemed extremely wise in the way he approached me. He began with compliments, sandwiched in what he thought might be negative information, and then concluded with a question. If nothing else, I knew this guy was smart! Within 15 minutes, I responded.

Wow...that is a good introduction, I must say! I will admit that this online stuff is new to me, so I feel a bit strange here, actually.

I've been divorced for almost three years and haven't "ventured out" yet. I've seen too many women make huge mistakes. Being in a leadership position in my church sort of restricts me from being too forward with any single gentlemen there, and I do want a gentleman!

Today is one of my days off, so I am doing great, and I have time to be on this crazy site, which, by the way, I haven't decided to pay for yet! Do you think it's worth it?

Gloria

Within 30 minutes, he replied.

Glad you wrote back. I've been on and off of here for maybe six months. Mixed results...I've even had my first stalker from here. That was awesome.

I get to Dallas occasionally, and by nature of my job have relocation opportunities available, so I've been open to a lot of different possibilities. Since you are in a visible position of leadership and living life in a fishbowl can be a bit of a challenge, this may be the perfect place for trying out your "dating legs."

So, if an idiot in tinfoil as opposed to a knight in shining armor might be intriguing to you, hit me with your best shot!

Seriously, I'd love to hear about your ministry!

Mike

O my goodness! Who was this guy? The only thing I remembered from his profile was that he was a Marine, and I must say that carried some credibility with me! He captured my attention as no one else had. No other messages even came close. I shot off a reply.

Mike,

Your ability to communicate (in writing yet!) indicates that you are more than an idiot, in tinfoil or otherwise! Unless, of course, you have your mother sitting next to you who is editing your work! That's the thing about this online stuff. What is real? Who is telling the truth? You've had your first stalker?

Help me out, here, so I don't have to keep checking your profile, which makes me feel like a stalker.

You live in Kansas?

You do what kind of work?

Do you have a criminal record?

I just moved to Dallas about two months ago, and I love it. Tell me what you know about Dallas!

His reply made me snicker.

Ouch! Mom doesn't like you anymore.

He answered all of my questions about where he lived and what he did for a living. He made sure to mention my beloved Arizona, that I had left to follow the call of the ministry. Then he answered the question I sort of asked tongue in cheek, although it also had some serious emotion behind it.

I travel to Phoenix every other month this year for a Masters program I'm in. I LOVE PHOENIX! Or Tempe to be more precise. I like the solitude and landscape of the desert.

As far as criminal records, I think I have two — Johnny Cash and Merle Haggard, although I haven't seen my Merle record for a while. (That was funny. I don't care who you are.) NO. I don't have a criminal record. You?

Who was this guy? He loves Tempe! That was my absolute favorite place to live! He made me laugh again! Who was this guy?

Within a day, I found out that he was a preacher's kid. His father felt called to attend Bible School in Joplin, MO, and when Mike was in fourth grade, his dad packed up the family and moved, much like I had done with my kids years before. He told me about his church background in some depth and his walk with the Lord. I was glad I didn't have to pry that information out of him.

If there was one thing I learned from my first marriage, it was to keep the yellow flag of caution up for a long time and always to have an escape plan while dating. Many people get married because they fall too hard too fast like I did the first time. As the wedding day approaches, either the man or woman becomes aware of character issues or personal proclivities that concern them, but the wedding's been scheduled, the family's been notified, and the gifts are already streaming in! How can they stop the matrimonial train that is barreling down the track to a lifetime commitment? Most people stay on the train. They dismiss the warnings, or they figure their future spouse will change. If you can't live with your intended precisely the way they are for the rest of your life, don't marry him/her!

Of course, people change over the years, but a person's essential character won't change. What he/she was taught as a child, what is important, what is right and what is wrong, can be hidden for a while, but it eventually makes its way out. Any person can overcome anything by applying the Word of God to his life, but it takes commitment and dedication. First, the person must admit that they need to change. That is often the most challenging step. After all, if mom and/or dad acted and thought a particular way, how could it be wrong? No one is chained to their parents' mistakes. Anyone can overcome anything by the blood of the Lamb and the word of their testimony *(Revelation 12:11)*. However, when choosing a spouse, I can't overestimate the influence their childhood had on them, and that is something that takes time to reveal.

So, while I was immediately smitten with this Mike guy who messaged me, I remained cautious. He gently suggested we exchange personal emails a day or two after we began communicating on the website. He acknowledged that men sometimes try to get women to communicate with them outside of the dating site so as to minimize competition. This guy, though, knew how to word things so nicely!

Listen, I know you are on here on a trial basis, and you may decide not to stay. I'm going to go out on a limb here and give you my personal email address. I've heard a lot of guys try to get a lady off of the site really fast for some reason; I guess to capitalize their time or something. Regardless, I know I enjoy talking to you and appreciate your wit and writing as well.

Okay, here goes. You ready? Wait for it...

His email came next. Then he closed with finesse, as usual.

There. Handle with care.

Mike

Once again, his writing engaged me as no one else's had. It wasn't only his words; it was his punctuation! Go ahead and laugh, but one of the things that impressed me most about this man was that he knew how to use a semi-colon correctly!

CHAPTER 18
Full Disclosure

As much as people may discount meeting someone online, I must say that when a relationship begins electronically in an appropriate manner, the two people involved can focus on important things. Think about it. If a woman meets a man for dinner, she tends to concentrate on his car, his haircut, his shoes, and the label of clothing he's wearing. When you meet someone online, you find out what's in their heart and mind before you can be distracted by such trivial things.

So it was with us. Our email interactions were non-stop. We covered every subject imaginable in depth. I would ask him questions — lots of questions; he would embed his answers and click *reply* usually within an hour. His answers were clear and honest. He was transparent yet considerate. Before long, I felt comfortable giving him my phone number. I remember hearing his voice for the first time. He had a little bit of a twang, almost as if he were a Texan, but he sounded strong — like a man who was comfortable with who he is.

We talked about our kids. He had four boys. The youngest was still in high school. The eldest and second-born were Marines. His 3rd had been in a traumatic car accident just months before. He was DOA when the medical helicopter picked him up. He had numerous surgeries on his leg and internal organs. His brain was without oxygen for several minutes, and the immediate prognosis wasn't good, but the community around them supported them, prayed, and God literally raised that boy from the dead. He was still in a rehab center when Mike told me about him. I knew without a doubt that this man loved his sons. He took his responsibility as a father seriously, and I respected him for that — another plus for this guy who used semi-colons correctly!

Since we had both been married before, I thought it was important to give him a little full disclosure about what it would be like to date me. Very early in our discussions, I told that no matter what, we would not engage in pre-marital sex. He wholeheartedly agreed. It seems funny to me that I brought that subject up before we even met in person, but we were getting deeply involved quickly, and I felt like the ground rules needed to be well established.

I felt like we needed to do something to slow things down a little, so I asked if he would read the book, *Too Close Too Soon* by Dr. James Talley. Dr. Talley, after years of counseling and study, concluded that after a certain number of hours together, an unmarried couple — even those with strong Christian morals and faith — will almost always succumb to the pressure of becoming physically intimate. The book suggests limited exposure to one another through the dating process so that you don't get caught in the *I want out but don't know how* syndrome.

Not only did this proper semi-colon wielding man immediately download the book to his iPad, but he also read it. Then he created a chart to track our time together. Dr. Talley's book was written before the Internet was very big, so he doesn't take into account how many emails a couple may exchange. Still, the point was that couples who get too close too soon should back off, slow down, and cool down to keep themselves from making a huge mistake. After digesting the book, Mike suggested that we limit our phone calls to twice a week. I had midweek services on Thursdays; so, he would call me on Wednesday and Sunday nights at 8pm.

I can hear some of you laughing! In retrospect, I am so thankful that he came up with that plan. It did several things for us. First of all, it gave us time to ourselves and our kids. Second, it gave me time to prepare for our calls. This may sound like I was a little compulsive, but I took the time to write out questions to ask him when he called. Then when he talked, I wrote down his answers. I wanted to see if his stories were consistent. I also wanted to have meaningful things to discuss and not just hem and haw and say how much we liked each other as two teenagers would! Third, it allowed me to see that he was a man who kept his word. My phone would ring at 8 on the dot! Not only could he punctuate; he was punctual! I was definitely falling in love!

After four weeks of emailing and talking on the phone, we decided to do a *communication fast* from one another. We took a week off from phone calls, emails, and texts. We still hadn't met in person.

Mike was scheduled to go to Phoenix in August for his Masters' class, and I thought it might be good for my friends to see him before I did. That way, if they assessed that he was a louse, a snake, and in general no good for me, I could break it off more easily.

I asked Mike if he would be willing to meet with my best friends there. I had known Bill and P.A. for over 30 years. We worked together, raised kids together, went to church together, sang in a quartet together, and traveled together. Before we moved to Detroit, we lived in the same neighborhood — only eight houses away — and we saw each other a lot.

I told them about Mike, and like everyone who cared about me, they were guarded.

Bill and P.A. are highly educated and not afraid of much; I knew Mike was the same. This meeting was bound to be interesting. They put him through the wringer, but in the end, my friends, still trying to remain impartial, said that he was extremely bright *(duh — he knows how to use a semi-colon!)*. They were impressed not only with his intellect but with his honesty and forthrightness.

They invited him to attend the church in Phoenix that we helped get off the ground almost 15 years earlier. My family was one of the first 12 members. I was the first worship leader and psalmist there, and Dean had a short stint there as an Assistant Pastor. Mike was a serious Christian, but he wasn't used to my type of church. After the service, he felt like he had to break our communications fast and call me.

We were both praying during the fast and seeking what God wanted us to do with our relationship. Instead of asking *if* we were to move forward or *why* we should move forward, Mike was asking God to show him *why not*. Maybe one of his *why nots* came into view that night. His visit to the church was uncomfortable. As a visitor, they asked him to stand up and then they sang him a song. But he's a Marine, and he'd dealt with worse than that. He survived the welcome song. The shouts of *"Hallelujah"* and *"Praise the Lord"* weren't part of his church culture, but by the end of service, he recognized the anointing and acknowledged that the people were genuine.

The *why not* of my unique church culture was abated. Mike discerned that he could handle it and was strong enough to be with me. However, he sensed that he had to allow me to get out of our relationship that night. He broke the communications fast and called me. He told me about his meeting with Bill and P.A. and the church service. Then he said, *"I know I'm strong enough to be with you, but the question I'm asking myself is, 'am I strong enough to let you go?' So, this is my attempt at being the strongest man you never met."*

That night we would decide to either move forward in our relationship or move on and meet someone else. We decided to move forward. He lived 8 hours away. Seeing one another in person would take much more commitment in time and money. He said he was willing to do it. He proved to me that I was worth pursuing, and I will always honor and respect him for that.

O Lord,
you have examined my heart
and know everything about me. You know
when I sit down or stand up. You know my
thoughts even when I am far away.
You see me when I travel, and when I rest
at home. You know everything I do.
You know what I am going to say even
before I say it, Lord. You go before me and
follow me. You place your hand of
blessing on my head.
Such knowledge is too wonderful
for me, too great for me
to understand!

Psalm 139:1-6 | NLT

CHAPTER 19
Too Good to be True

Mike bought a plane ticket and flew to Dallas for Labor Day weekend for our first meeting. I arranged to take half a day off — officially — I filled out the forms and everything, but my position didn't really have time off. Our visit was interrupted by a barrage of texts about getting a floor buffed. One of my superiors didn't want me to spend the money on it. Another of my superiors insisted I get it done. I was the pickle in the middle, and it was not a good introduction to what life with me might be like! Amid all of the work texts, Mike and I still got a lot accomplished.

Wisely, before he came to visit, he asked if there was anything I needed to be done around the house. I'm a single woman! Of course, there was! I needed him to help me put all of my moving boxes in the attic. I was sure to move again, so I didn't want to throw them away. It was well over 90 degrees that day, and Mike trudged up and down the stairs into the uncooled attic until I could fit my car in the garage.

Since I knew he was coming, I figured I might as well get as much work out of him as I could, so I ordered two rocking chairs for my porch. They came in a box and needed assembly.

He also offered to grill dinner. However, since I didn't have a grill, we had to pick one up at Home Depot, which of course, he also had to assemble.

I don't know if he knew it yet, but acts of service is my love language, and he was speaking it fluently!

Ebeth was in Dallas that weekend and got to meet Mike. She was appalled at how much work *"I made"* him do. He brought his guitar with him and began to strum something as I cleaned up from dinner. Ebeth came sliding into the room, grabbed a large spoon for her microphone, and began singing an ad-lib song. Mike was seriously impressed with her. I'm not so sure what she thought about him.

A few weeks earlier, when I told her I had met someone on the Internet, she wasn't happy. She thought I had lost all sensibility and was engaging in dangerous behavior. She had done everything in her power to protect me and help me through the crisis, and she wanted to shield me from making another big mistake. I assured her that we hadn't met yet. He lived far away and that he *"was a good man."* Every time I would describe him to someone, I would say, *"He's such a good man."* At the time, my daughter wasn't so sure.

By the end of the weekend, I wasn't feeling well, I was stressed from work, and I just wasn't sure about this guy. He was terrific, but the littlest things bothered me. Ridiculous stuff like his socks, for example. Yes, his socks.

I never thought about what kind of socks my "prince charming" would wear, but I didn't think he would wear what Mike had on inside of his cowboy boots: ankle socks. For some reason, I expected him to wear Calvin Klein dress socks with cowboy boots. Never having known anyone who wore boots almost exclusively, I didn't understand that wearing half socks was normal. I was obviously looking for reasons to not like him. Nonetheless, he could tell I was getting cold feet (no pun intended).

Before I drove him to the airport, Mike told me he recognized that I wasn't ready, and I wouldn't hear from him again. I was relieved; at least I didn't have to be the one to end it.

I dropped him off at the airport, and we hugged one another. Then I got on the road for a 3-hour drive to Austin. I was teaching in the Bible school there that week. As soon as I got on the freeway, I began to sob. As odd as this may sound, it was if my spirit was crying, not just my emotions. Deep inside, I knew that man was sent to me from God, and I just pushed him away.

One of my concerns was that this was all too good to be true. I hadn't even dated another man. I thought he was right for me, but what if I was simply settling for the first one who showed interest? I had to be sure that I wasn't jumping into something and missing something better.

Thankfully, he called me again about something he had done to help a friend of mine in Dallas, and we began to talk again. I finally told him how I felt. Up to that point, I had guarded my mouth and not said anything that would indicate any commitment or attraction to him. But now, he knew. I also told him that I wanted to be sure. I hadn't dated anyone else or even had any meaningful conversations with any other man. I wanted to go back on that Christian singles' site for ten more days. He agreed. He was wise to acknowledge that I needed to be certain.

I went back on the site and engaged in conversation with only one other gentleman — a professor from Ohio. But honestly, he had two strikes against him from the start. First, he lived in Ohio. He said he was willing to relocate, but understanding tenure in Universities, I knew that was highly improbable. I was born in Ohio, and as much as I enjoyed it as a child, living there as an adult never appealed to me. Second, he had a 16-year-old daughter. It's one thing to marry a man with sons; it's another thing to try to compete with a girl's love for her daddy. However, it could work, so we messaged each other through the site and set a time for him to call me. Our conversation was stilted. We just didn't click. I knew then what I knew before; I just didn't want to admit it. Mike was the man for me.

Later I learned that during the ten days that I went back on that site, Mike did too — but not to look for women. He looked at the men in my geographical area and prayed. I'm not sure how he prayed, or if I could recommend his prayers as Biblically sound! Nonetheless, he had put our relationship in God's hands. It wasn't too good to be true. It was so true that it was of God, and it was very good.

CHAPTER 20
Telling My Pastor and Family

I love my pastor. He did more for me through this crisis than anyone. He could have simply kicked me to the curb when the crisis hit. My last name was a liability to him, but he didn't see me that way. He viewed me as an anointed minister of the Gospel in my own right. He respected me for the way I raised my kids, and he knew that my relationship with Jesus was legit.

My pastor is a very dignified individual who has accomplished great things. He founded a church in the Detroit area, which at one time had over 20,000 members. He was a Detroit city councilman from 1990-1994 and was the only Republican on the council since 1965. As a man of African descent, his decision to change parties in the 1980s was not popular with many of his congregants and neighbors in Detroit, but he is a man of principle. If he thinks something is right, he will do it regardless of commentary, backlash, or bad press. He was raised, like most African Americans in Detroit, to be a Democrat, and that's what he was until he read the party platforms in the early 1980s and compared them to the standards of God's Word. He will be the first to tell you that God is not a Republican. Nor is He a Democrat, but as a Bible-believing Christian pastor, he couldn't overlook his party's support and promotion of abortion. He made an unpopular decision, and I respect him highly for doing what he thought was right according to God's Word. My pastor lives according to the Bible to the best of his ability. I could never have any other kind of pastor because that's the way I live too. We haven't always seen everything eye-to-eye, but I know his decisions are based on his understanding of WWJD *(What would Jesus do)*. Do people still wear those bracelets?

One of the things we didn't agree on was the issue of online dating. We never spoke about the issue one-on-one, but he made comments from the pulpit that indicated his opposition to it. Perhaps his negative take on it came from hearing horror stories of women who were sexually assaulted and killed by men they met online, and out of an abundance of caution, as a good shepherd would, he wanted to protect (particularly) the women of his congregation.

By the middle of September, I wanted to let my pastor know about Mike. After we met in person, broke up, and got back together, Mike drove 8 hours to see me the weekend of September 28. He spent the day and early evening with me but retired to his own hotel room at night. We played Scrabble (I think he let me win), went to dinner at my neighborhood restaurant (where I used to go try to look available), and he attended the church where I worked, albeit incognito. I still hadn't introduced him to my pastor, and both of those important gentlemen deserved a proper introduction to one another. Mike and I talked about how to do it. My pastor was also my boss, so much was at stake. I figured my pastor's first inclination would be to reject Mike, out of concern for me, so approach mattered.

Had I just come out and said, *"I met this man online,"* I knew the reaction would not be positive, and I would have to dig myself out of a very deep hole. Mike took the lead. He composed an incredibly honest and articulate letter of introduction. He described our online connection by saying that we met through an organization that is linked to Focus on the Family. An entirely true statement — the *Christian Cafe*, being Christian in more than name only, had a link to Focus on the Family as a relationship resource. He talked about his work, his church background, his education, his boys, and his relationship with the Holy Spirit. Lest you think I overdramatize this man's ability to write, let me share the closing statement of his letter of introduction to my pastor.

I am a common man, sir. A common man that is blessed to know an extraordinary woman. I tell you these things to ask your blessing on our commitment to seek our future together in a way that honors, respects, and protects her, her commitment to your ministry, and the name of our Lord Jesus Christ.

How could I not love this man?

Mike sent the letter to me, and I hand-delivered it to my pastor several days later. He sat in my office and read the letter. His comments were sparse, but not much different than what I expected.

"He's a PK, huh?"

"He's divorced? You'll have to find out about that."

Then his closing words that day to me were, *"You're old enough to know about puppy love, so we'll see if he's still around in a few months; then I'll talk to him. But I'm not surprised. If it's not him, I knew it would be somebody."*

If there's one thing I know about my pastor, it is that he prays, and he hears from God. I believe he went home that night, re-read the letter of introduction, prayed about this man, and God spoke to him because the *few months* turned into *pretty soon.* He came into my office the next day and told me he was going to call Mike and let him know that he wouldn't try to keep me in Dallas if I needed to move to Kansas City. I assured him that I was planning on staying; Mike's company had employment opportunities in the Dallas area. My pastor finished our conversation that day by saying, *"You're both over 50 years old. I trust your judgment. I'll stay out of this unless you need my counsel."*

A few days later, while I was visiting my parents in Phoenix, my pastor called Mike. Mike said they had a few good laughs together and that my pastor was very encouraging. During that trip to Arizona, I told my parents about the man I met online. My dad surprised me.

"I've already heard all about him. Bucky called me and gave me the scoop!"

Bucky Woy was my father's long-time friend from Akron, Ohio, who moved to Dallas decades ago. He and my dad were both involved in the sports business.

My father, an unknown name, is considered by some to be one of the most influential people in the history of golf. He was one of the founders of Golf Pride grips, the rubber golf grip that is used by about 90% of touring pros today. In the late 1940s, living in what was then the *rubber capital of the world,* a wealthy industrialist from Cleveland found my dad and his partner in their fledgling rubber business that did contract work for B.F. Goodrich. He documented the development of the Golf Pride grip in a short memoir, which is a fun and enlightening read.[5] Bucky Woy was a sports agent for Lee Trevino and some other high-profile athletes. He and my dad were old friends, and he was the only person outside of my church that I knew in the gigantic metroplex of Dallas.

When Mike visited me for the first time, I was uncomfortable with him staying at a hotel for a few reasons. First, since my pastor didn't know about him yet, I didn't want to risk running into someone from my church as I was meeting a man in a hotel lobby for lunch or picking him up to take him to the airport. Second, I wanted someone I knew to meet this guy I met online. I didn't want to tell my pastor yet, but at the same time, I didn't want to enter into a relationship without anyone knowing anything about him.

Bucky and his precious wife, Mitzi, graciously opened their lovely home to a complete stranger from Kansas City because their old friend's 53-year-old daughter asked them to! I wondered if they would think I was crazy; most people my age would just get a nice hotel room — and probably share it with their newfound love interest. But Bucky and Mitzi are Christians, and they understood my odd request. My parents, in their late 80s by this time, didn't travel any longer, but evidently, Bucky called my dad on a reasonably regular basis. He let my dad know that Mike seemed to be a good, honest, hardworking, and intelligent guy.

My parents were very cautious with their words. They never bad-mouthed

---

[5] Junker, Bill, the History of the Golf Pride Grip-A Nostalgic Commentary (Newark: Ralph Maltby Enterprises, 1989)

Dean. They knew I was married to him for 30 years, and two of their precious grandchildren were his offspring. They also guarded their comments about Mike. They didn't want to be responsible for leading me down the wrong path or derailing me from the right path. They trusted my intelligence and wisdom, albeit the mistakes I made in my past. My father was a man of few, but always well-chosen words. His smile when he talked about his conversation with Bucky indicated he was on board with my relationship with Mike. My mother was thrilled that I found someone who could *"take care"* of me.

On the same visit to Phoenix, I spoke to my best friends who had taken Mike through the gauntlet with an interview and a visit to our Phoenix church just a few months earlier. Their first reactions to me were like my parents' — very cautious. However, once I let them know that Mike and I were convinced we were to move forward with our relationship, they revealed the truth about their impression of him. Bill admitted that after he met with Mike the first time, he told his wife, *"He and I could be friends,"* but he didn't want to tell me at the time because he didn't want to influence my decision.

Telling my daughter was a different story. I remember talking to her in the living room of my little rented house in Dallas. As much as she knew I needed to move forward, I think she wanted me to find someone that was a known commodity — someone who was a part of our church circle, perhaps.

The idea that I was getting into a serious relationship with a guy I met online was traumatic to her. She cried. I cried. I don't blame her. She loved her dad and her mom. I can't imagine what her heart and soul were going through. I tried to console her that I wasn't making a stupid mistake. This was a good man. (Again, I used that phrase nearly every time I described him to anyone because he truly is a good man!) Our pastor knew about him; Bill and P.A. (her Godparents) had interviewed him and approved of him. Furthermore, I had not left God out of the decision; I had been praying about this since we began talking, as had Mike.

At the end of October, I flew to Kansas City for an extended weekend visit on Mike's home turf. We drove to the quaint town of LaCygne, Kansas where Mike had been living in a small place he and his boys fondly referred to as *the shanty*. It was deserving of the name, but it was a great little place for a bachelor and his two nearly-adult sons. His second son, Aaron, decided he liked me almost immediately. His sage and somewhat sarcastic advice to his father was, *"Don't screw this up."* His youngest son was still in High School, and I'm sure that he didn't know how to react to me. I remember watching Mike deal with some issues with his boys, and I could tell he was a very good dad.

I met the pastor whom Mike said knew his name when I questioned him about his walk with the Lord in one of our first emails. He was surprised, I think, when Mike told him I was a pastor, but he spoke highly of Mike, and that's all I needed to hear.

On our way to Branson, Mike got to hear me burst out praying in tongues as he took a dangerous curve in the dark on the edge of a cliff. It didn't scare him away, so we carried on. After all, he is a Marine!

He rented a room at a nasty but inexpensive hotel, but I stayed in the summer lake home of some friends of his. Of course, we spent our days together. Mike had planned our trip well. He took me to Missouri's theme park — Silver Dollar City — which has a strong Christian foundation. A chapel sits on the main pathway of the theme park, and as we passed, I saw a sign announcing *Hymn sing-alongs* at various times throughout the day. I was thrilled and insisted we attend. Mike is a bass player, not a singer, but he acquiesced to my request. I was so impressed that he knew all of the verses to all of the hymns. I had to sight-sing most of them since I came from the Catholic church (that had their own hymns) and then went to churches that did contemporary music. Most of the songs were new to me, but this guy knew every single hymn! It was such an endearing experience. His faith was deeply rooted. His parents took him to church every time the doors were open when he was young, and it showed!

We visited the College of the Ozarks, also known as *Hard Work U* — a Christian university where students "pay" their tuition through work. On the campus, we visited the museum of the Ozarks where I got to see the original vehicle the Beverly Hillbillies drove when they *"moved to Beverly — Hills that is — swimming pools, movie stars."* We ate a lovely lunch at the high-end restaurant on site that is staffed by college students paying for their education through work.

These were *his people* — hard-working, authentic, patriotic, men and women, who loved family and faith. I never had a close relationship with anyone from *flyover country,* but I began to realize that they held the same values I did. They didn't focus on outward appearance; few people there considered having facelifts or tummy tucks. They knew what was important in life and they enjoyed the simple things — sweet tea on the porch in the summertime, roaring fires in the winter, and family meals after church on Sundays. Although I had lived my life pretty much as a city girl, I connected with the values of these people who lived in unknown towns and small cities in the middle of our country.

While in Branson, we attended Friday night service at Keith Moore's Faith Life Church. I had been there before, but no one knew me, yet it was as if I had a *"Pastor"* sign on my head. Their first-class ushers led Mike and me right down to the front row. I was used to sitting in the front row and felt odd anywhere else, but Mike was the opposite. He had to adjust to being front and center, but after all, he's a Marine. He dealt with it and enjoyed the service.

I met his parents on that trip too. They were aware that he was involved with a *pastor lady* he met online, but like most of the people who loved me, they were cautious. I remember his dad telling Mike, *"Be careful."*

Mike had expressed such great respect for his father that I looked forward to meeting him. He's the reason Mike knows how to do almost everything. He took his eldest son to work when he was overseeing the facilities at Ozark Christian College in Joplin, Missouri. As a ten or twelve-year-old boy, Mike learned to weld, build, and fix almost anything. His dad is a car guy who taught his sons to change oil, fix brakes, and just about anything else on a motorized vehicle.

I loved listening to Mike and his dad as they sat at the kitchen table and talked about his kids, life, and a variety of other topics over their morning coffee. His dad, who had served his church in many capacities since graduating from *Ozark Christian College,* was the administrator of a Christian Senior facility at the time. He was in his late 70s and still working hard! He treated his wife like a queen and cared about her every need. Mike's mother was sweet and welcoming, but I'm sure she was thinking, *"We shall see."* After all, they are from Missouri — the *show me* state.

CHAPTER 21
Preparing for a Second Marriage

Oddly, I don't remember when Mike asked me to marry him. I recorded the day he gave me a beautiful, almost full carat, nearly perfect diamond ring. On that day, he posed the perfunctory question, but we had decided long before, that, unless something came up that was a clear sign to cut it off, we were preparing to be married, and we intended to make it work. Although we were not yet officially engaged, by March of 2013 (6 months after we met), we were planning to be married.

There's a lot of misinformation about the percentage of Christian marriages that don't make it *'til death do us part.* About 50% of first marriages in the United States end in divorce, but contrary to a popular headline, the divorce rate amongst serious Christians is not as high as the general population. Being a committed believer, attending church regularly, and sharing your faith with your spouse does make a difference in your odds for marital success. A recent study by Harvard trained researcher, Shaunti Feldahn, showed a much lower divorce rate among active Christians — around 20%.[6] But I always say that statistics only matter if you're not one of them; if you're one of the 20%, your odds are 100%! Mike and I were both part of that 20% in our first marriages, but we were determined that our second marriage wouldn't be. We were willing to prepare to succeed.

---

[6] https://www.1.cbn.com/cbnnews/us/2014/June/Church-Divorce-Rate-Way-Lower-than-Anyone-Thought

Being separated by almost 600 miles allowed us to focus on important things, which is vital if a couple is preparing to marry. When a couple dates in the same city, they often become almost like married people — not only sexually — but in conversations that tend to be less and less interrogative and more and more superficial.

We were continually questioning one another about our values and standards. A few months after we began talking, Mike suggested we both create a document that outlined our expectations, boundaries, goals, and traps. Here is how he described the exercise and its purpose.

This document has been created as a resource or "scratchpad" for detailing four areas of relationship that need definition. Finding the components of these areas and drilling down through them to find agreement, in my opinion, will help create the foundation we build on in a practical fashion. The assumption must be made that spiritual growth and kingdom service will always be a driving factor at any level of relationship. These items are not the only areas of relationship that need to be defined, but they are meant to be a good starting point for definition.

We both listed our expectations, boundaries, goals, and traps and discussed them at length. Could we support each other's goals? Were our expectations realistic? Could we maintain the proper boundaries and avoid the traps that could derail our relationship with each other, our families, our churches, and our Lord?

Mike's *scratchpad* was our first formal marriage preparation program, but more was to come! As an ordained pastor, I had a library full of resources, and I wasn't afraid to use them. After reading and implementing the plan from *Too Close Too Soon*, we read *Marriage on the Rock* by Jimmy and Karen Evans. Then we read *Saving Your Second Marriage Before It Starts* by Drs. Les and Leslie Parrott. We both purchased a copy of the workbook that the Parrotts produced with their book; we read and answered questions privately, and then shared them on our facetime visits.

Some of the topics we covered were: remarriage readiness, your personal ten commandments, communication, and his and my top ten needs.

We would have submitted to pastoral counseling, but my pastor had told me he trusted me. He was available if we wanted counsel, but he wouldn't require it. I don't suggest this for everyone. Most people should have pastoral counseling before marrying. However, we were staying accountable. Both of us had consistent interaction with my pastor, and we were doing at least as much, if not more, than most couples do to prepare on our own. We were determined to not be part of the 20% of failed Christian marriages again!

In April, Mike drove down to attend our church picnic. He helped grill the burgers and hot dogs as I stayed busy overseeing the entire event, volunteers, and staff. Before the picnic was over, Mike and my pastor pulled away from the crowd to have a man-to-man talk. Of course, everyone noticed! One of the staff ministers asked me, rhetorically with a smile on her face, *"Well, I wonder what's going on over there!"*

Mike had sent another letter earlier that month to my pastor telling him we intended to be married. He asked for my pastor's blessing and for him to officiate the ceremony. I wasn't part of the conversation, but Mike told me that my pastor filled him in on some things about my situation, and nothing surprised him. We had covered it all. My pastor gave his blessing and agreed to officiate at our second wedding, where we vowed to make it *'til death do us part.*

CHAPTER 22
Wedding Planning the Second Time

When I was a 21-year-old bride, my precious parents blessed me with a beautiful, and I'm sure quite costly wedding. They weren't the country club type, but they joined the hard-to-get-into Arizona Country Club a few years before I wed. I never discussed it with them, but I can't help but think they joined primarily to have a place for my inevitable wedding because shortly after I was married, they dropped their membership. The men rented tuxedos; the bridesmaids wore matching formal dresses. We had hors d'oeuvres, an open bar, a catered dinner, a live band, and a wedding cake of several flavors. I insisted on carrot cake, but my mother felt we should also have the traditional white and chocolate cake available. It was beautiful. I'm sure it was expensive.

Thirty-four years later, I was planning my second wedding This one was on our nickel, and we proved that it's possible to have a memorable event without spending a lot of money. There were no tuxedos, no formals for the bridesmaids, no country club, no band, and one kind of cake. I bought my wedding dress from a Chinese dress company that sold on Amazon. It cost under $100. Thankfully, I was pleasantly surprised at the quality of the dress, although it was too big. My days as a single woman had reduced me to somewhere between a size 0 and a 2, and I paid more to have it altered than I did to buy it!

I didn't want to be married in the building where I worked. It just didn't feel right. I looked online and found an event venue that was a cute little old farmhouse about 45 minutes north of Dallas in the small town of Melissa, TX. It's called *The Bird's Nest,* and it seemed like the perfect place for me to marry a man who was from the country. I didn't care much about having the perfect event. I just wanted to get married! I did choose theme colors of yellow and purple simply because I consider them to be "happy colors," and I was happy!

Like most places these days, they offered a discount if you held your event Monday-Thursday. So, of course, since this was a budget wedding, we got married on Thursday. I insisted that we abide by my church's strong recommendation to date for at least one year before marrying, and we complied, but just barely! We met on July 19, 2012, and we married on July 25, 2013. Tables and chairs were set up on the lawn, and the ceremony took place on the back porch. We prayed for cool temperatures and got them. It was July in Texas, but it wasn't unbearable.

My daughter and my daughter-in-law were my bridesmaids. In keeping with the country theme, they wore cowboy boots and a simple purple dress that cost under $20. My three granddaughters were all flower girls. I found their dresses on Amazon too. They were inexpensive and beautiful.

Two of Mike's sons were in the wedding. Nate served as an usher and Aaron, in his Marine dress blues, looked amazing standing next to his father as a best man. Mike bought a new gray suit; it wasn't anything very expensive but was decent quality. My dear friend from Round Rock, Donna, found us a beautiful tie that coordinated Mike's suit to the theme colors. We purchased matching ties for my son, who walked me down the aisle, and my soon-to-be son-in-law, who also served in the wedding party.

My daughter was engaged to be married shortly after Mike and I announced ours. She got married the following January. Although I was buying my dress from Amazon, and a dear friend made hers, we visited a bridal store on one of her trips to Dallas and tried on wedding dresses together. It was something I never expected to do with my daughter, but it was fun and memorable!

Marrying a sound technician has its advantages. Mike put together a lovely playlist for before, during, and after the ceremony. He also arranged for a microphone for the officiant. We served a buffet of heavy hors d'oeuvres, but no steak, salmon, or chicken dinner or alcohol. My daughter was a thoughtful maid of honor and brought me a plate, but I couldn't eat much. I was too excited!

Instead of a formal guest book, I bought a paperback copy of the children's book, *The Country Mouse and the City Mouse* for people to sign. Anyone who was there understood its meaning: it described the groom and the bride perfectly.

Except for Mike's iPad's background playlist, we didn't have any entertainment, but there was a bit of unplanned show during the toasts. As is customary, the best man and maid of honor offered a few words to honor the bride and groom. Aaron said some nice things about his dad and ended jokingly with, *"Well, Gloria, now he's your problem."* When it was Ebeth's turn, we were surprised to see her take a seat. Mike was even more startled when he saw her with his guitar that we had left at the house! In true Ebeth style, instead of speaking a toast, she sang a special little ditty she composed as she drove to Dallas for the wedding. She said,

"This is for you, Mike and Mom. Happy wedding day." Then she sang

My momma's getting married today

To a man who used to live around hay — Mike Brintnall.

They met on the Internet;

I wasn't too sure about that until I met him one day.

I knew that he loved you when you told me all the things he did for you.

What did he do? Well he

Built two rocking chairs, put together a grill to share, cleaned out your garage.

Read a million books for you;

Raked the yard 'cause you asked him to.

Mike Brintnall, you are — the man of my momma's dreams.

You bought her a big fat diamond ring.

She knows you can do anything.

Mike Brintnall you are — the man of my momma's dreams.

Her song was perfect. Everyone chuckled, including Mike and me. It was completely true. He did everything she said, except the number of books I asked him to read was a *bit* exaggerated.

Mike and I were tremendously encouraged and blessed that Bill and P.A., who put him through the interview gauntlet in Phoenix almost a year earlier, drove to Dallas to be with us on that day. So did our dear friends from Round Rock, Stu and Donna. They helped in so many ways – setting up and tearing down – oh, and Bill may have saved the groom's life by performing the Heimlich maneuver on him! We were enjoying a steak dinner the night before the wedding when Mike suddenly became very quiet. He had a piece of steak caught in his throat! Thankfully, Bill noticed, knew what to do, and did it!

I want to apologize publicly to all of our friends and family who attended our wedding. First of all, I am so sorry that I asked you to drive on US 75 northbound from Dallas to Melissa during rush hour! I rarely ventured outside of my little neighborhood by Love Field, and I had no idea how horrid traffic was. God bless you for enduring it to attend our nuptials!

Second, I hope we didn't rush you through our reception, but we were sort of in a hurry to get out of there, if you know what I mean.

You saw me before I was born. Every day of my life was recorded in your book. Every moment was laid out before a single day had passed. How precious are your thoughts about me, O God. They cannot be numbered! I can't even count them; they outnumber the grains of sand! And when I wake up, you are still with me!

Psalm 139:16-18 | NLT

CHAPTER 23
Grief Affects Belief

Now that you've read the story, I want to teach a little about practical and Biblical things you can do when *stuff happens* to you so that you come out on the other side better, not bitter.

Mike and I are living happily ever after. Life is still life. We continue to work, pay bills, and fight off colds, aches, and pains. We've dealt with some challenges since we were married, but we are truly happy. We love and honor one another. We are tremendously grateful that God brought us together, despite our mess-ups and mistakes. We are serving God in our marriage, our family, our jobs, and our church. I am happier than I ever thought was possible. I call him, *The Amazing Mr. Mike Brintnall* because to me, that is precisely what he is.

My story is unique, but so is yours.

Regardless of who you are, how much money or influence you have, or what you know, *stuff* happens. There will inevitably be a moment when something transpires that is so shocking, so sudden, and so life-altering that you will feel as if the rug has been pulled out from under you. Your feet will falter; you will fall on your face, and you will grieve. Everyone will grieve over *something* at some time.

It might be news of a loved one moving to heaven.

Or maybe you get a call from your son, daughter, or spouse who tells you they need a lawyer — and fast.

It could be getting fired after serving faithfully at your job or in a ministry for many years.

Maybe the money you thought you had saved for a rainy day suddenly disappears when the investments you thought were secure turned out not to be.

It might be getting a diagnosis from a doctor that includes the word, *terminal*. Or it could be the day you realize that the marriage you believed was *'til death do us part* is over.

People expect you to grieve when a loved one dies, but grief can come from any significant life-altering event. Grief is *serious mental suffering or distress over affliction or loss. It is sharp sorrow or painful regret.*

I grieved the loss of my 30-year marriage, the break-up of our family, the closing of the church I co-pastored, the ruin of my reputation, and the pain it brought to my children. The onion of grief that my pastor friend in Lubbock had described to me was revealing its layers.

My pastor was a great counselor for me, but since he was also my boss, I thought it might be wise to talk to someone else as well. I found a Christian family counselor through my health insurance and made an appointment. She gave me a paper with the seven stages of grief listed: shock, denial, anger, bargaining, depression, testing, and acceptance. She asked, *"Which stage are you in?"*

I knew it had been too soon for her to believe I was at the acceptance stage, but I was no longer in shock, denial, anger, bargaining, or depression. Maybe testing? I was still learning how to live on my own and dealing with adjusting to the single life, so perhaps that was it.

I was looking for the *Praise the Lord anyway* stage, and it wasn't there! I knew one thing for sure. I definitely experienced grief, but I wasn't going to plant myself in any of those stages for very long. Instead of grief, I held onto belief — in God and His Word.

Life on this earth comes with problems, hurt, and pain. Even people of great faith admit that Jesus Himself said, *In the world ye shall have tribulation: but be of good cheer; I have overcome the world. (John 16:33)*

We often bring troubles on ourselves through bad decisions and wrong actions, but sometimes we are blindsided. Although we pray and do everything we knew to do, sometimes *stuff* just happens that radically affects our lives in a negative way. Dreams are shattered. Reputations are destroyed. The loss brings grief, and if we get stuck in one of the stages of grief for too long, it will affect our belief. Even the men who walked with Jesus for three years weren't immune to the faith-robbing effects of grief.

When we read the Bible, we often think that the people who followed Jesus were some kind of super-people. But they weren't. Have you ever stopped to think about how they felt when Jesus was crucified? Put yourself in their shoes. Walk through that day in your mind; consider what they saw, heard, and felt as they watched the One they called *Rabbi* and *Lord* suffer. They never expected this. Jesus didn't cause any trouble with the Romans. He paid His taxes. He fed thousands, healed the sick, and raised the dead. He was innocent, but they were unable to help the One they loved.

And the soldiers led him away into the hall, called Praetorium; and they call together the whole band. And they clothed him with purple, and platted a crown of thorns, and put it about his head, And began to salute him, Hail, King of the Jews! And they smote him on the head with a reed, and did spit upon him, and bowing their knees worshipped him. (Mark 15:16-19)

And they bring him unto the place Golgotha, which is, being interpreted, The place of a skull. And they gave him to drink wine mingled with myrrh: but he received it not. And when they had crucified him, they parted his garments, casting lots upon them, what every man should take. And it was the third hour, and they crucified him. (Mark 15:22-25)

And when the sixth hour was come, there was darkness over the whole land until the ninth hour. And at the ninth hour Jesus cried with a loud voice, saying, Eloi, Eloi, lama sabachthani? which is, being interpreted, My God, my God, why hast thou forsaken me? (Mark 15:33-34)

There were also women looking on afar off: among whom was Mary Magdalene, and Mary the mother of James the less and of Joses, and Salome; (Who also, when he was in Galilee, followed him, and ministered unto him;) and many other women which came up with him unto Jerusalem. (Mark 15:40-41)

How do you suppose the women at the cross reacted? I'm sure they were all weeping. They were most likely overcome with grief.

Jesus' followers expected Him to lead a rebellion against Rome. They saw Him raise Lazarus from the dead; they gave up their businesses to serve Him. They loved Him, but on that Friday, they saw Him scourged, beaten crowned with thorns, spat upon, and nails were driven in His hands. He was stripped of His clothing and His dignity as He was lifted up for all to see, and He cried out in agony to the Father, *"Eli, Eli, Lama Sabachthani."*

Jesus' followers weren't prepared for this, although Jesus told them it would happen, they didn't understand. Maybe they thought, like many of us, that if we're following God, we will be immune from pain and sorrow. But that's not what Jesus promised.

Verily, verily, I say unto you, That ye shall weep and lament, but the world shall rejoice: and ye shall be sorrowful, but **your sorrow shall be turned into joy.** *(John 16:20)*

Just as Jesus prophesied, they wept; they lamented, and the world rejoiced. They were sorrowful, but their sorrow was turned to joy. It took a few days, but it came to pass just as He said!

At the end of the sabbath, as it began to dawn toward the first day of the week, came Mary Magdalene and the other Mary to see the sepulchre. (Matthew 28:1)

And the angel answered and said unto the women, Fear not ye: for I know that ye seek Jesus, which was crucified. He is not here: for he is risen, as he said. Come, see the place where the Lord lay. (Matthew 28:5-6)

And they departed quickly from the sepulchre with fear ***and great joy;*** *and did run to bring his disciples word. (Matthew 28:8)*

The women who grieved at the cross ran from the tomb with *great joy* when they encountered the risen Lord, but the men didn't believe the women's story about the risen Lord.

Now when Jesus was risen early the first day of the week, he appeared first to Mary Magdalene, out of whom he had cast seven devils. And she went and told them that had been with him, as they mourned and wept. **And they, when they had heard that he was alive, and had been seen of her, believed not.** *After that he appeared in another form unto two of them, as they walked, and went into the country. And they went and told it unto the residue: neither believed they them. (Mark 16:9-14)*

The men *believed not.* They hadn't seen Jesus. They were still grieving the loss of their Lord. Their grief affected their belief, and it does the same thing to people today. Even committed Christians often doubt God when they go through periods of grief. Every believer will have a time or two in life when Satan, whose purpose is to steal, kill, and destroy *(John 10:10)* does his very best to steal your joy, kill your hope, and destroy your faith.

It's not a sin to grieve, but grief should be temporary. *Psalm 30:5* is true. It says, *weeping may endure for a night, but joy cometh in the morning.* Grieving is not meant to be a way of life. Satan wants you to remain in mourning so that you can't utilize all the benefits of salvation.

Joy, not mourning, is what draws out all that Jesus paid for on the cross — healing, deliverance, peace, prosperity, and the ability to be led by His Spirit!

Therefore with joy shall ye draw water out of the wells of salvation. (Isaiah 12:3)

Don't allow grief to rob you of belief — in God, in what He's done for you in Christ, in His love for you, in His Word, or in His future for you.

You may have hit a bump in the road, but you can get past it with faith in God. A well-known evangelist used to say, *"You don't have any problems. All you need is faith in God."*

If you are grieving today, you may think this sounds harsh and unsympathetic, but honestly, faith is the victory *(1 John 5:4)* — over anything. There is a time to cry, but how long that lasts is really up to you.

To appoint unto them that mourn in Zion, to give unto them beauty for ashes, the oil of joy for mourning, the garment of praise for the spirit of heaviness; that they might be called trees of righteousness, the planting of the Lord, that he might be glorified.

Isaiah 61:3 | KJV

CHAPTER 24
From Mourning at Night to Joy in the Morning

I remember the heaviness of those first days when I was in shock, the first stage of grief. I couldn't eat or sleep. I didn't cry. It was as if I was wandering around in a haze carrying a 100-pound backpack. But that only lasted a short while. Although the legal and emotional challenges continued for months, I was back on the path toward joy very quickly. It took a little longer than *overnight* as *Psalm 30:5* says, but I went from mourning to joy within a few weeks. In retrospect, I can pinpoint a few attitudes, convictions, and practices that helped me climb out of the pit of grief and self-pity.

First, I didn't feel guilty about grieving. I knew that Jesus understood. *Isaiah 53:5* says that Jesus was *a man of sorrows and acquainted with grief.* The word *sorrows* in the original Hebrew text means *a pain — physical and mental.* Grief is mental and emotional pain. God is not angry when you are sad. Jesus experienced grief, and He never displeased the Father.

When news of my situation became public, a dear friend sent me a miniature decorative bottle with the following Scripture on a piece of paper inside:

You keep track of all my sorrows.
You have collected all my tears in your bottle.
You have recorded each one in your book. (Psalm 56:8 NLT)

God knows. God sees. God cares. And God will carry you through to the other side.

Second, I was old enough, mature enough, and familiar enough with the Bible to understand that *stuff* happens, but it's always temporary. Nothing lasts forever. I was confident that there was joy on the other side.

When my father told me, *"Buck up; you'll get through this,"* he was reminding me that nothing — even the worst situation in the world — lasts forever.

Psalm 23 may be the most well-known Psalm of the Bible. It likens God to a shepherd and His people to sheep. It describes the provision, peace, and protection He gives us. Verse 4 says, *Yea, though I walk through the valley of the shadow of death, I will fear no evil.* Too many people get *to* the dark valley, but they don't continue *through* it. Keep walking. Keep moving forward; don't stop! You will get out of the mess!

Years before the crisis hit, I memorized *Hebrews 12:2-3.* I often recited it to myself when dealing with difficult people and situations in the ministry. And believe me, I had plenty of opportunities to quote it!

Fixing our eyes on Jesus, the pioneer, and perfecter of faith. For the joy set before him, he endured the cross, scorning its shame, and sat down at the right hand of the throne of God. ³Consider him who endured such opposition from sinners, so that you will not grow weary and lose heart. (Hebrews 12:2-3 NLT)

When stuff happens that causes grief, think about Jesus. He endured opposition from sinful men to the point of death on the cross. Don't get weary! Don't lose heart! Jesus thought about you and me and millions of other people who would become part of God's family while He hung on the cross and died. He looked past the pain to the joy.

Look toward something better that lies ahead for you! I understood that I was in a battle. The devil wanted to rob me of my joy, which I needed more than ever because *the joy of the Lord is [my] strength. (Nehemiah 8:10)*

Third, I convinced myself that I could be joyful even in the worst possible circumstances. I chose not to have the stereotypical response to my problems. Too many times, people react to situations the way they see actors deal with them in movies or soap operas. They create a scene. They cry. They scream. They throw things. They get drunk. Instead, I decided to rejoice in God!

You might have read my story and thought, *"She didn't have it so bad. You should hear what I've been going through."* Yes, your situation may be much worse than mine, but you can come out of it victoriously! Even if everything is gone, you can still choose joy! Consider what the prophet Habakkuk said.

Although the fig tree shall not blossom, neither shall fruit be in the vines; the labour of the olive shall fail, and the fields shall yield no meat; the flock shall be cut off from the fold, and there shall be no herd in the stalls: Yet I will rejoice in the Lord, I will joy in the God of my salvation. (Habakkuk 3:17-18)

I might not have had as severe a problem as you, but you probably don't have it as bad as Habakkuk! He didn't have anything, but he chose to rejoice in the Lord. Regardless of what I was facing, God was still God.

He hadn't moved, changed, or altered His character. He was still good. He was always love. He was bigger than anything I was facing.

Our culture tries to mold us to fit their expected behavior. For example, if a loved one dies, people expect you to be morose, down, depressed, sad, and gloomy. If you rejoice at the Funeral home, people don't know how to react. They may think you're in denial or shock; it may be viewed as disrespectful, but it is possible to sorrow and rejoice at the same time. The Apostle Paul wrote *We then, as workers together with him, beseech you also that ye receive not the grace of God in vain...As sorrowful, yet always rejoicing. (2 Corinthians 6:2,10)*

How was Paul able to rejoice in his sorrow? He suffered much more than most of us ever will. Do you remember what he endured for the sake of the Gospel?

Of the Jews five times received I forty stripes save one. Thrice was I beaten with rods, once was I stoned, thrice I suffered shipwreck, a night and a day I have been in the deep; In journeyings often, in perils of waters, in perils of robbers, in perils by mine own countrymen, in perils by the heathen, in perils in the city, in perils in the wilderness, in perils in the sea, in perils among false brethren. (2 Corinthians 11:24-26)

First, Paul knew that the *stuff* he had to endure didn't come from God, but from demonically influenced people *(messengers of Satan)* who were trying to get him to close down his ministry — much like they did with me.

And lest I should be exalted above measure through the abundance of the revelations, there was given to me a thorn in the flesh, the messenger of Satan to buffet me, lest I should be exalted above measure. For this thing I besought the Lord thrice, that it might depart from me. (2 Corinthians 12:7-8)

God answered me when I cried out to Him in much the same way He answered Paul. He didn't miraculously make all my problems disappear; He gave me the grace to get through them.

And he said unto me, My grace is sufficient for thee: for my strength is made perfect in weakness. Most gladly therefore will I rather glory in my infirmities, that the power of Christ may rest upon me. (2 Corinthians 12:9)

Grace is the empowerment of God. When I didn't feel like I could go on, God empowered me. He reminded me of His love and faithfulness. I chose to rejoice in Him alone, not in any outward manifestation of good fortune.

Consuming God's Word brought me joy despite my sorrow, just as it did for the prophet, Jeremiah.

Thy words were found, and I did eat them; and thy word was unto me the joy and rejoicing of mine heart. (Jeremiah 15:16)

I wasn't about to stop consuming God's Word when I needed His joy the most! Instead of letting the problem eat me, I ate God's Word. It was my source of strength, and it produced a joy that few could understand.

Before my world came crashing down, I had been praying in the Spirit every day for long periods for many years. I believe I went from mourning to joy quickly because of my fellowship with the Holy Spirit; when He comes on the scene, He brings joy.

At that same time Jesus was filled with the joy of the Holy Spirit. (Luke 10:21 NLT)

I've heard it said that there's no such thing as a sad Holy Ghost. Wherever you see the Holy Spirit mentioned in Scripture, you see joy, power, wisdom, or comfort. He is the Comforter. *(John 14:16)*

When *stuff* happens that is entirely life-altering, it's often difficult to even know how to pray. Praying by the power of the Holy Spirit allows you to pray God's perfect will in the situation — even when you don't have a clue what it is.

Likewise the Spirit also helpeth our infirmities: for we know not what we should pray for as we ought: but the Spirit itself maketh intercession for us with groanings which cannot be uttered. And he that searcheth the hearts knoweth what is the mind of the Spirit, because he maketh intercession for the saints according to the will of God. And we know that all things work together for good to them that love God, to them who are the called according to his purpose. (Romans 8:26-28)

Christians often quote *Romans 8:28* to encourage one another through difficulties, but they neglect the two preceding verses. All things work together for the good for those who love God and are called according to His purpose because they have prayed God's perfect will by praying in the Spirit. God's will doesn't automatically happen on the earth. John Wesley famously said, *"God does nothing except in response to believing prayer."* Remember that God gives everyone free choice. He doesn't force His will on anyone. He is waiting to help you; all you have to do is pray. When you pray in the Spirit, you pray effectively and powerfully, and all things will work together for your good!

At least a year before my personal crisis, I put aside an hour a day to do nothing but pray in tongues. It took some discipline. I didn't do laundry, clean, or go through papers on my desk while I prayed. Ironically, I can still recall walking around our guest bedroom (which also served as my office) praying aloud upstairs while my husband was downstairs in his rather secluded and dark office. Sometimes it bothered me that he was down there doing who knew what while I was feverishly interceding. Now I know why. Still, I was praying by faith, and I was praying out my future. I didn't realize at the time what my future held, but the Holy Spirit did. I am absolutely convinced that the hours I prayed in the Spirit prepared the way for my daughter and me to escape the trap the enemy set to destroy us emotionally and spiritually.

After all the *stuff* happened, I had to take my eyes off of myself — at least once in a while — and look for someone I could help. I knew that *Psalm 41:1* promised that when you help the poor, God will deliver you in trouble. I was in trouble. I needed to be delivered. I found some people who were worse off than I to help.

I always reminded myself that, regardless of how difficult my situation was, I knew other women were going through worse. I found some that were and slipped them a little cash. I gave to a ministry that assists families of incarcerated individuals. God's Word promises that sowing in tears would result in reaping in joy!

They that sow in tears shall reap in joy. He that goeth forth and weepeth, bearing precious seed, shall doubtless come again with rejoicing, bringing his sheaves with him. (Psalm 126:5-6)

Finally, I was cautious about who I let comfort me. Job told his buddies, *"miserable comforters are ye all." (Job 16:2)* They were terrible comforters because they assumed the worst about Job. They didn't bring him any hope or encouragement. They simply pointed out what they thought were his failings. As my dear mother used to tell me when a girl would talk smack about me, *"Gloria, with friends like that, who needs enemies?"* I spoke to people like my sister, who believed in God and me. I knew I didn't need to be continually rehashing the problem with people. I looked for those who would talk about the future and the good things God was doing in our lives.

I had some excellent, faith-filled counseling, but honestly, most of my comfort came from the Holy Spirit as He spoke to me through God's Word. As the Scriptures promised, *weeping endured for a night, but joy came in the morning!*

CHAPTER 25
Five Ups for When You're Down

We all go through *stuff* in life, but to move forward, we must get out of the *poor, poor pitiful me* syndrome. You might be familiar with it as *nobody knows the trouble I've seen* attitude. The Bible tells us that whatever your problem, you are not the only one who has had to deal with it.

If you think you are standing strong, be careful not to fall. The temptations in your life are no different from what others experience. And God is faithful. He will not allow the temptation to be more than you can stand. When you are tempted, he will show you a way out so that you can endure. (1 Corinthians 10:12-13 NLT)

God always makes a way out of any temptation, trial, or tribulation!

A few years after all the stuff happened, I asked God how I got through it so well. I knew it wasn't because I had ministerial credentials in front of my name. Lots of people with much more impressive titles and letters after their names than me have been physically and emotionally wrecked from an unexpected crisis. *"How did You get me through, Lord?"* I wondered.

God is gracious and kind. He showed me that the way out of a pit is always up. I didn't know it at the time, but I did five "up" things that helped both me and my daughter get through the mess and end up with a message of hope. Some of these are spiritual. Some are very natural.

First, I filled up with the Word of God.

I had spent years studying the Bible before everything happened. I had been putting the Word in my heart and speaking it out of my mouth for decades before the crisis hit. I didn't have to run to my computer, do a Google search or call my pastor to find Scriptures that reminded me that God loved me or that promised me a hope and a future. I was confident about God's love for me.

Do you remember what I said when my daughter asked me what was going on? I wanted her father to tell her, and I wasn't even clear on what was happening, I just knew it wasn't good, and our lives would be forever changed. I didn't scream, *"Oh my God! I don't know what is happening!"* I didn't fall into her arms and sob. I simply said, *"Everything's going to be okay. Jesus still loves us."*

I wasn't trying to be inspirational or deep. I truly believed it because I had the Word of God firmly embedded in my heart. Knowing God's Word is knowing God's character. I knew that I knew that I knew that God so loved me that He sent Jesus to die for me, and since He didn't hold back His only Son, He would take care of me. I knew He was faithful. He said He would never leave me nor forsake me.

My pastor uses the analogy of a tube of toothpaste to describe being filled up. When it is squeezed, toothpaste comes out because someone, in a factory somewhere, put toothpaste in the tube. When life inevitably squeezes you, whatever you've put inside is what will come out. If your first words are cuss words, that's because that's what you've filled yourself with.

If you wait to fill up until you're squeezed, it will be too late. Fill up when you aren't in a crisis situation. It's much easier to fix a leaky roof when it's sunny than when it's raining. *Out of the abundance of the heart, the mouth speaks. (Luke 6:45)* Fill up with the Word of God so you will speak words of life even in the most challenging situations.

Second, I was linked up with my pastor.

Thankfully, I wasn't a wandering Christian. Sheep who roam without a shepherd are called *lunch* for the wolves. *Ephesians 4:11-12* tells us that God gave us pastors. If He gave them, we must need them. Ten years ago, online churches were pretty rare, but today a lot of people say they belong to an online church. You might attend church via the Internet and hear a famous preacher weekly, but when the going gets rough, he or she will not be there to walk with you through the battle. Even if the online church offers some phone counseling, which can be effective at times, you need someone who knows you and your situation. You need someone who won't be afraid to tell you the hard truths. You might need someone to literally hold your hand for just a moment like I did when I got the shocking news about what I was facing.

I am grateful that my pastor helped me make the right decisions because most people make bad decisions when they are in the middle of a battle. I needed a pastor for the same reason a platoon needs a platoon leader. The platoon leader tells the soldiers when to march and when to hunker down. He directs which weapons to use and how and when to shoot. Too many people get in the battle of their lives, and they don't look to their pastor for direction and wisdom. They end up using the wrong weapon, or they shoot at the wrong time or in the wrong direction. They may take friendly fire. Without proper leadership, they hunker down when they should be marching and move when they should be standing still! Don't be a casualty of war because you go it alone. Link up with a pastor. I honestly don't know what I would have done without my pastor. If you've been church hopping or afraid to commit to a pastor, I want to encourage you to link up now.

Third, I showed up.

I showed up at church and showed up daily for my prayer and Bible study. Listen, there were times, particularly at first, when going to church was horribly uncomfortable for me. One of my first Sundays in Round Rock, a visiting preacher announced from the pulpit, while I was sitting in the second row, that the church I had been pastoring was closed due to moral failing of the pastor. What he said was absolutely true. I did wish he would have warned me so I could have slipped out before the announcement. I felt like every eye in the room zoomed in on me. I wanted to run, hide, and never show my face again. But praise God, I didn't have much choice. My church was also my place of employment. Still, there were days I didn't want to show up. Another time a precious lady, trying to comfort me, said, *"Well, you know everyone thinks it's the wife's fault for not 'giving it up' for her husband. But I know better."* Her comment made me a bit uncomfortable, to say the least.

Hebrews 10:25 says that we are not to forsake *the assembling of ourselves together, as the manner of some is; but exhorting one another: and so much the more, as ye see the day approaching.* In other words, the tougher the times get, the more you need to get yourself to church! Times were tough for me, so whether I liked the way I thought people were thinking about me or not, I showed up.

There were also mornings that I didn't want to take the time or effort to pray and read the Bible before I left for work. I was physically exhausted, especially those first few weeks, but I always showed up. I have a "prayer chair" that's been with me since my son was an infant. I would sit in that chair every morning. Some days I would eloquently praise, worship, intercede and supplicate. Other days about all I could say was, *"Good morning, Lord. I love you. Help me."* God spoke to me in that prayer chair. He encouraged me, strengthened me, and gave me the direction that I desperately needed, but I had to show up.

Fourth, we turned up. (The *Urban Dictionary* defines *turn up* as *party time.*)

I'm not talking about sinful partying, as many associate with this *Urban Dictionary* phrase, but my daughter and I purposed to find things to celebrate. We were on a tight budget, but we had a fast food place near us that had half-price milkshakes after 8pm. Every Thursday, after our midweek church service, we got milkshakes together. We were doing *Nehemiah 8:10: Then he said unto them, Go your way, eat the fat, and drink the sweet, and send portions unto them for whom nothing is prepared: for this day is holy unto our Lord: neither be ye sorry; for the joy of the Lord is your strength.*

We made sort of a big deal out of it. We got to know the guys who worked the drive-through on Thursday nights. They knew I usually ordered a coffee milkshake and she usually got chocolate. We looked forward to Thursday nights. When we were both working so hard to keep our heads above water, we took a break and gave thanks with half-price milkshakes! It encouraged our joy and helped us finish the week strong! We turned up with our milkshakes on Thursdays.

Finally, I looked up.

I focused on God and gave Him thanks. *1 Thessalonians 5:18* says, *in everything give thanks for this is the will of God in Christ Jesus concerning you.* I didn't thank God for the problem; I thanked Him in the midst of it! He was still God! He always loved us. He gave us everything we had, even if it wasn't as much or as good as what someone else had or what we had before, without God, we wouldn't have anything good. There is always something to be thankful for. *Psalm 34:1* was my mantra: *I will bless the Lord at all times. His praise shall continually be in my mouth.* Yes, I would respond to questions with *Psalm 34:1*. I'd sing praise choruses when I wanted to cry or scream. I would randomly blurt out while driving in the car, *"Bless the Lord, O my soul!"*

CHAPTER 26
H.O.P.E. = Have Only Positive Expectations

I couldn't have come out of my mess as quickly or as thoroughly as I did without faith. Faith is fundamental to the Christian life. *Romans 1:17* and *Habakkuk 2:4* tells us that the *just shall live by faith.* Most believers understand that they are saved by grace through faith. *(Ephesians 2:8)* Faith moves mountains *(Mark 11:23),* and faith is the victory that overcomes the world. *(1 John 5:4)*

One of the first Scriptures I memorized was *Hebrews 11:1: Now faith is the substance of things hoped for, the evidence of things not seen.* Faith is now. Faith is the manifestation of what you have hoped for. Faith is evidence. I knew the lines of all the famous *faith preachers.* I incorporated many of them in my preaching. I had been part of *Word of Faith* circles in the body of Christ for decades, but the only thing I ever heard about hope was that it wasn't faith. People who thought they were in faith were often only in hope, and that's why they weren't able to *say unto the mountain, be thou removed, and be thou cast into the sea. (Mark 11:23)*

Hope isn't the victory. Faith is. Hope, for many years, was rather maligned amongst preachers of faith. In the last few years, some have begun to mention hope in a more positive light, but it still seems to be a bit of a mystery.

I love hope. Without hope, faith has nothing to give substance to. Hope is the prerequisite of faith. When I was in the darkest days of my life, a tiny light of hope blazed in my heart.

For me, hope was the pilot light of faith. Let me explain. When I lived in a small apartment in college, we had a gas stove with a pilot light. I didn't try to cook on the pilot light, but I knew that without the pilot light, I couldn't cook at all. In the same way that the pilot light didn't produce enough heat to cook my meal, hope didn't have enough heat to move mountains, but hope kept burning in my heart, and it eventually fired up my faith.

Some dismiss hope because they equate it with wishing. But Bible hope is much more than a wish. Bible hope means *to anticipate with pleasure, expectation, or confidence.*

English speakers, however, often use the words *hope* and *wish* interchangeably. For example, someone might say, *"I hope I win the Publisher's Clearinghouse Sweepstakes."* It would be much more accurate to say, *"I wish I would win the Publisher's Clearinghouse Sweepstakes,"* because the odds of winning are infinitesimal. They are about the same, whether one enters or not. Therefore, I cannot hope (in the Biblical definition of the word) to win because it is impossible to have a *confident expectation* of winning.

It was pointless for me to *wish* that stuff didn't happen, but I was empowered knowing that with God, I had a confident expectation that something better was yet to come.

H.O.P.E. became my tagline. It stands for Have Only Positive Expectations. Sure, my life was shockingly upended, but my life wasn't over. I was still alive, so God must have had a future for me. The Old Testament prophet expressed God's hope for Israel when he wrote, *"For I know the plans I have for you," declares the Lord, "plans to prosper you and not to harm you, plans to give you hope and a future." (Jeremiah 29:11 NIV)*

It's interesting to note that the Hebrew word for *hope* that Jeremiah used is *tiqvah*. It means a *cord*. Hope was the rope that connected me to faith.

When I was in a deep, dark hole of despair, I didn't know how to get out. I didn't know what was outside of the hole, but I grabbed onto the rope of hope and hung on. Eventually, it pulled me up to ground level where I could move forward!

I may not have been in faith, but I was in hope. I knew something good was on the other end, although I couldn't see it or define it. When you're going through tough stuff, you are often in the dark; you just don't know what you just don't know. I didn't know that I would become one of the first females with the title of *Pastor* in our large church organization. I didn't know that I would meet and live happily ever after with the Amazing Mr. Mike Brintnall, who lived two states away at the time. I didn't know I'd write this book and tell this story all over the world. I just had hope — a positive expectation that *something* good was in my future simply because I knew that God loved me.

Faith, hope, and love are *"God's big three"* because *I Corinthians 13:13* says, *Three things remain forever — faith, hope, and love — and the greatest of these is love (NLT)*.

Faith is the substance of things hoped for, but hope is the evidence of knowing God's love.

When my world came crashing down, when my life was suddenly altered, when I didn't know what I would do or how I would recover, I still knew one thing: God loved me. Maybe at that point in life, I didn't believe I could move a mountain, but I did believe the love of God.

And we have known and believed the love that God hath to us. (1 John 4:16)

When the negative stuff happened, I didn't need to pretend I was a *Strong's Concordance,* quoting a hundred Scriptures with the Greek and Hebrew or have a three-minute confession memorized. But I absolutely, unequivocally, without any restraints declared with boldness, *"God loves me!"*

Faith works by love, Galatians 5:6 tells us, but too many Christians try to be in faith without being in love. Of course, we must love others for our faith to work, but more importantly, we must know that God loves us!

Faith is a Bible word for *trust,* and when you are assured of someone's love, you can trust him or her, can't you? When I taught my children to swim, they willingly jumped off the edge of the pool into my arms because they knew I loved them. They trusted me. My love would not let them drown.

I knew that God loved me. The Creator of the Universe cared for me! He would not let me sink in the mud of my mess! I leaned on His love. I believed His love. I responded to His love. I sang about His love. I reminded myself that the God of Abraham, Isaac, and Jacob, the First and the Last, the Almighty, Elohim, El Elyon loved little ol' me!

What shall we then say to these things? If God be for us, who can be against us? He that spared not his own Son, but delivered him up for us all, how shall he not with him also freely give us all things? Who shall lay any thing to the charge of God's elect? It is God that justifieth. Who is he that condemneth? It is Christ that died, yea rather, that is risen again, who is even at the right hand of God, who also maketh intercession for us. Who shall separate us from the love of Christ? shall tribulation, or distress, or persecution, or famine, or nakedness, or peril, or sword? As it is written, For thy sake we are killed all the day long; we are accounted as sheep for the slaughter. Nay, in all these things we are more than conquerors through him that loved us. For I am persuaded, that neither death, nor life, nor angels, nor principalities, nor powers, nor things present, nor things to come, Nor height, nor depth, nor any other creature, shall be able to separate us from the love of God, which is in Christ Jesus our Lord. (Romans 8:31-39)

I don't know what you may be facing now or in the future; regardless of what it is, God is for you. He is on your side, and nothing can separate you from His love except you! It's up to you to connect to His love and stay there! Love *never gives up, never loses faith, is always hopeful, and endures through every circumstance. (1 Corinthians 13:7 NLT)*

You may not know how, and you may not know when you will get out of the situation you are facing today, but hope says *sooner or later, one way or another, you will get to something better simply because God loves you.*

God is love. He never gave up on me; He never left me. He is the God of H.O.P.E. because He has only positive expectations for me — and you!

EPILOGUE

It took me ten years to write this book. We are still navigating new waters when it comes to dealing with the situation and all the stuff that happened a decade ago.

After serving the federally mandated 85% of his sentence, Dean was released from prison. Sadly, like many incarcerated Americans, he entered society with nothing. Ebeth had an old car that Mike rebuilt for her dad. I kept a checking account with his name on it so he could show some history with a bank over the last ten years, and Mike and I put a little money in it for him. After several months of searching and applying, he finally found part-time employment. I continue to pray for him. He is the father of my children, and I respect him for his part in raising such amazing, strong, anointed kids. Please keep him in your prayers. I want the best for him.

Mike has met with him and hears from him via text message periodically. I am still not comfortable being around him. Some suggest that I haven't forgiven him; I don't believe that is the case. I have nothing but sympathy and compassion for him.

I know that God loves Dean, and therefore, he too can H.O.P.E. With God, nothing is impossible.

As for me, God has indeed turned my mourning into dancing. He has put off my sackcloth and clothed me with joy. *(Psalm 30:11)* I am one incredibly grateful woman.

Prayer

Hope will get you through the darkest situations, but you've got to know the God of hope first. Contrary to popular opinion, there are not many ways to know Him. Jesus said, *I am the way and the truth and the life. No one comes to the Father except through me. (John 14:6)*

Jesus died on the cross because God loves you. He rose from the dead so that you could live forever in heaven. When you say out loud, *"Jesus is Lord,"* and believe in your heart that God raised Him from the dead, you become a child of God. Pray this prayer and connect with the God of H.O.P.E.:

Father, I believe You sent Your Son, Jesus, to die on the cross for my sins. I believe You raised Him from the dead. I turn away from sin and to You. Come into my heart, Holy Spirit, and make me a brand-new person – full of HOPE and peace and joy, in Jesus' name. Amen.

Congratulations! Your future is bright! God Has Only Positive Expectations for you. I can't promise that you won't encounter more *stuff* in life, but I can promise you that God's Word has the solution for every situation.

About the Author

Passionate, candid, and compelling, Gloria Brintnall's ministry focuses on God's big three – faith, hope, and love. She has lived a life of faith for nearly 40 years.

Titles don't mean much to her; she's been called Pastor, Minister, and Reverend. In over 20 years of full-time ministry, she has been a worship leader, Bible school instructor, staff minister, itinerant preacher, church planter, assistant pastor, and pastor.

Her favorite and most influential titles are those of wife and mother. Her two adult children are both serving God in full-time ministry. Her daughter is an anointed worship leader, youth pastor, and Christian vlogger. Her son pastors Faith4life church in Carrollton, TX, where they good-humoredly call her the *"Reverend Mother."* She currently assists in a leadership and preaching capacity at his church, travels to other churches bringing a solid, Spirit-filled and Bible-based message of hope, and serves other ministries as a ghostwriter creating newsletters, books, and articles. She's lived in lots of places, but for now, she and her husband, the Amazing Mr. Mike Brintnall, make their home in the outskirts of Dallas. Together they have 6 children and 5 grandchildren. To book Gloria for speaking engagements or personal appearances, connect with her at gloria.brintnall@gmail.com.

OTHER BOOKS
By Gloria Brintnall

How to Never Fail for Parents –
Applying 1 Corinthians 13 to Raising Children

~

Twenty-One Days to Seal Your Zeal –
How to Stay Fired up without Burning Out

~

Hitting the Bullseye of Faith when Crisis Hits You

AVAILABLE AT

Amazon.com | gloriabrintnall.com | gloria.brintnall@gmail.com